Tapas

The food and the music

Parragon

Bath · New York · Singapore · Hong Kong · Cologne · Delhi · Melbourne

This edition published in 2009

Parragon
Queen Street House
4 Queen Street
Bath BA1 1HE, UK

Produced by the Bridgewater Book Company Ltd.

Internal design by Talking Design

ISBN: 978-1-4075-4838-8

Printed in China

Notes for the Reader
This book uses imperial, metric, and U.S. cup measurements. Follow the same units of measurement
throughout; do not mix imperial and metric. All spoon measurements are level; teaspoons are assumed
to be 5 ml and tablespoons are assumed to be 15 ml. Unless otherwise stated, milk is assumed to be
whole, individual vegetables such as potatoes are medium, and pepper is freshly ground black pepper.
Recipes using raw or very lightly cooked eggs should be avoided by infants, the elderly, pregnant
women, convalescents, and anyone suffering from an illness. Pregnant and breastfeeding women are
also advised to avoid eating peanuts and peanut products. The times given are an approximate guide
only. Preparation times differ according to the techniques used by different people and the cooking
times may also vary from those given.

Contents

Introduction

ONE OF THE MANY DELIGHTS OF VISITING SPAIN IS THE RICH TRADITION OF TAPAS. THE ORIGIN OF TAPAS IS UNCLEAR, BUT ONE LEGEND HAS IT THAT TAPAS WAS FIRST COOKED FOR KING ALFONSO X, KNOWN AS EL SABIO ("THE WISE"), THE RULER OF CASTILE IN THE THIRTEENTH CENTURY. THE KING, SUFFERING FROM AN ILLNESS, WAS REQUIRED TO CONSUME SMALL QUANTITIES OF FOOD AND WINE BETWEEN MEALS. ON HIS RECOVERY, HE ADVOCATED THAT WINE WAS NOT TO BE SERVED IN INNS WITHOUT SOMETHING MORE SOLID TO ACCOMPANY IT.

HOWEVER, MOST CONSIDER THAT ANDALUSIA, NOT CASTILE, CAN LAY CLAIM TO BEING THE BIRTHPLACE OF TAPAS. IN THIS FAMOUS WINE-MAKING REGION, IT BECAME CUSTOMARY TO SERVE WINE IN A GLASS COVERED BY EITHER A SLICE OF BREAD WITH HAM OR CHEESE, OR A SAUCER CONTAINING SOME OTHER FOOD. THIS "TAPA," A WORD WHICH MEANS A "COVER" OR "LID," ACTED AS A BARRIER TO PREVENT FLIES OR OTHER IMPURITIES FROM CONTAMINATING THE WINE, AND IT WAS NOT LONG BEFORE THE DISH ITSELF BEGAN TO BE KNOWN AS A "TAPA." FROM THIS STARTING POINT, TAPAS SPREAD THROUGHOUT SPAIN, AND NOW BEYOND.

In contemporary Spain, tapas remains an essential and integral part of Spanish lifestyle, usually served between lunch and dinner in cafés and bars with an aperitif, such as wine, sherry, or cider. This provides an ideal stopping point for people returning home in the evening, and also offers friends and colleagues the chance to unwind at the end of the day. Alternatively, choosing a larger number of dishes can turn the event into an entire meal. The broad variety of tapas reflects these differing needs, cosas de picar ("little things to nibble") being the simplest finger food—a bowl of olives, say, or salted nuts—and pinchos, slightly larger fare, which is speared on a toothpick. At the other end of the scale are raciones, which are larger dishes that can form the basis of a more filling meal.

The range of tapas dishes is vast and is a reflection of the variety of culinary traditions of the different Spanish regions. This book presents a selection of some of the most famous dishes, such as the classic

Spanish Tortilla (see page 100) and Tomato Bread (see page 240), as well as lots of regional specialties such as "Wrinkled" Potatoes in Mojo Sauce (see page 24) from the Canary Islands and Traditional Catalan Salt Cod Salad (see page 124), served in bars in Barcelona.

Tapa is no longer the preserve of Spain, with numerous tapas bars and restaurants springing up in cosmopolitan cities throughout the world. It is also becoming increasingly popular to make and enjoy at home.

Part of the appeal of tapas is that eating them can be one of the most social ways of dining with friends and family, particularly when eaten as an entire meal, with everyone sampling the wide range of dishes at the table. The fact that so many hot and cold dishes can be eaten alongside each other also makes it one of the more eclectic eating experiences. It is not often that you can take a couple of bites of a fish dish before sampling a chorizo empanadilla, all accompanied by a glass of wine and a few marinated olives. You can let your taste buds guide you to whatever sort of dish you fancy next!

Key ingredients

CHEESE

There are numerous cheeses produced in Spain, though the vast majority are limited in availability to the region where they are produced. Manchego, made from sheep's milk, is probably the most well known Spanish cheese and is widely available. Many other Spanish cheeses are used in the recipes in this book, but acceptable, more common substitutes are also suggested.

CHORIZO SAUSAGE

Chorizo is one of the best known and most widely available Spanish sausages. It is made from pork (smoked or unsmoked) and seasoned with paprika. It can be bought in various different sizes and with varying quantities of fat.

GARLIC

Garlic is a key ingredient in Spanish cooking. Garlic bulbs should be stored in a cool, dry place, and once a head of garlic has been broken into, the cloves should be used within 10 days, before they dry out. When buying garlic, look for firm heads with a tight, white outer skin.

HAM

Ham is a staple of Spanish cuisine, and hams have been produced for at least 2,000 years. The quality of ham is dependent on the maturation period, and the best hams, the most expensive, are often hand-sliced. They are suitable for being served raw as tapas. Less expensive ham should be cooked. Italian prosciutto can be used instead. Serrano ham is a generic term for cuts of leg meat from pigs from the mountain regions. These hams are salt-cured and breeze-dried.

OLIVE OIL

Spain is the largest producer of olive oil in the world, so it is no surprise that it is also the cornerstone of Spanish cuisine. The best quality olive oil is extra virgin, which is the first cold pressing and should be saved for dressings and marinades rather than used for frying. Virgin is less refined than extra virgin. A blend of virgin and refined oils is known simply as "olive oil," though it is not as widely exported as the other varieties.

OLIVES

It is perhaps no coincidence that olives, a staple of tapas and eaten alone or in more complex dishes, are a key produce of Andalusia. Over half of the 50 varieties of olive grown in Spain for eating come from this region. Some dishes in this book use olives stuffed with pimiento—a large, heart-shape sweet pepper.

PAPRIKA

Spanish paprika, the finely ground powder of dried sweet red pepper, is normally milder than the central European paprika, though occasionally much hotter varieties are used.

Basic Recipes

FRIED POTATOES

SERVES 6

2 lb 4 oz/1 kg potatoes,
  unpeeled
olive oil
sea salt

1 Scrub the potatoes and pat them dry, then cut into chunky pieces.

2 Put 1/2 inch/1 cm olive oil and 1 potato piece in 1 or 2 large, heavy-bottom skillets over medium–high heat and heat until the potato begins to sizzle. Add the remaining potatoes, without crowding the pans, and cook for 15 minutes, or until golden brown all over and tender. Work in batches, if necessary, keeping the cooked potatoes warm while you cook the remainder.

3 Use a slotted spoon to transfer the potatoes to a plate covered with crumpled paper towels. Blot off any excess oil and sprinkle with sea salt. Serve immediately.

TOMATO & BELL PEPPER SALSA

MAKES 1¼ PINTS/700 ML

4 tbsp olive oil
10 large garlic cloves
1 cup chopped shallots
4 large red bell peppers, seeded and
  chopped
2 lb 4 oz/1 kg ripe, fresh tomatoes,
  chopped, or
2 lb 12 oz/1.25 kg good-quality canned
  chopped tomatoes
2 thin strips freshly pared
  orange rind
pinch of hot red chili pepper flakes,
  to taste (optional)
salt and pepper

1 Heat the olive oil in a large, flameproof casserole over medium heat. Add the garlic, shallots, and bell peppers and cook for 10 minutes, stirring occasionally, until the bell peppers are softened but not browned.

2 Add the tomatoes, including the juices if using canned ones, orange rind, hot chili pepper flakes, if using, and salt and pepper to taste, then bring to a boil. Reduce the heat to as low as possible and simmer, uncovered, for 5 minutes, or until the liquid evaporates and the sauce thickens.

3 Purée the sauce through a mouli. Alternatively, purée in a food processor, then use a wooden spoon to press through a fine strainer. Taste and adjust the seasoning if necessary. Use immediately, or cover and let chill for up to 3 days.

Vegetables

THE RECIPES IN THIS CHAPTER ARE A MIXTURE OF VEGETABLE AND VEGETARIAN DISHES THAT ARE A DELICIOUS BITE-TO-EAT IN THEIR OWN RIGHT, AND OTHERS THAT WOULD MAKE GREAT SIDE DISHES TO SOME OF THE RECIPES CONTAINED ELSEWHERE IN THIS BOOK. THERE IS A WIDE VARIETY OF POTATO DISHES—ALWAYS A STAPLE OF TAPAS MENUS—INCLUDING THE EVER POPULAR BABY POTATOES WITH AÏOLI (SEE PAGE 12) AND THE CATALAN CLASSIC, FEISTY POTATOES (SEE PAGE 15). AS ITS NAME SUGGESTS, THE LATTER USES A HOT SAUCE TO SPICE UP FRIED POTATOES WITH AÏOLI.

OTHER TAPAS DISHES INCLUDE THE DELIGHTFUL, BITE-SIZE STUFFED CHERRY TOMATOES (SEE PAGE 38), THE SLIGHTLY MORE SUBSTANTIAL ZUCCHINI WITH CHEESE & VINAIGRETTE (SEE PAGE 43), AND A RANGE OF TASTY SALADS.

Spanish Potatoes

SERVES FOUR

2 tbsp olive oil
1 lb 2 oz/500 g small new
  potatoes, halved
1 onion, halved and sliced
1 green bell pepper, deseeded
  and cut into strips
1 tsp chili powder
1 tsp mustard
1¼ cups strained tomatoes
1¼ cups vegetable stock
salt and pepper
chopped fresh parsley
  to garnish

1 Heat the olive oil in a large, heavy-bottom skillet. Add the new potatoes and sliced onion and cook, stirring frequently, for 4–5 minutes, or until the onion slices are soft and translucent.

2 Add the bell pepper strips, chili powder, and mustard to the skillet and cook for 2–3 minutes.

3 Stir the strained tomatoes and vegetable stock into the skillet and bring to a boil. Reduce the heat and let simmer for 25 minutes, or until the potatoes are tender. Season to taste with salt and pepper.

4 Transfer the potatoes to a warmed serving dish. Sprinkle the chopped parsley over the top and serve immediately.

5 Alternatively, let the potatoes cool completely and serve cold, at room temperature.

New Potatoes with Chili Sauce

SERVES FOUR-SIX

1 lb/450 g new potatoes,
  unpeeled
2 garlic cloves, chopped
2 dried red chilies, lightly
  crushed
1 tbsp paprika
2 tbsp sherry vinegar
²⁄₃ cup olive oil
salt

VARIATION: You can substitute 1 deseeded and finely chopped fresh red chili for the dried chilies if you prefer. Stir it into the sauce at the end of Step 2.

1 Place the potatoes in a steamer set over a pan of boiling water. Cover and steam for 30 minutes, or until tender.

2 Meanwhile, make the sauce. Place the garlic, chilies, and paprika in a mortar and grind to a paste with a pestle. Season to taste with salt, then gradually work in the vinegar. Finally, work in the olive oil.

3 Transfer the potatoes to warmed serving dishes and serve immediately, handing round the chili sauce separately.

Baby Potatoes with Aïoli

SERVES SIX–EIGHT

1 lb/450 g baby new potatoes

1 tbsp chopped fresh
   flatleaf parsley

salt

AÏOLI

1 large egg yolk, at room
   temperature

1 tbsp white wine vinegar or
   lemon juice

2 large garlic cloves, peeled

5 tbsp Spanish extra-virgin
   olive oil

5 tbsp corn oil

salt and pepper

1 To make the Aïoli, place the egg yolk, vinegar, garlic, and salt and pepper to taste in a food processor fitted with a metal blade and blend together. With the motor still running, very slowly add the olive oil, then the corn oil, drop by drop at first, then, when it begins to thicken, in a slow, steady stream until the sauce is thick and smooth. Alternatively, use a bowl and whisk to make the Aïoli.

2 For this recipe, the Aïoli should be quite thin to coat the potatoes. To ensure this, blend in 1 tablespoon of water to form the consistency of sauce.

3 To prepare the potatoes, cut them in half or fourths to make bite-size pieces. If they are very small you can leave them whole. Place the potatoes in a large pan of cold salted water and bring to a boil. Reduce the heat and simmer for 7 minutes, or until just tender. Drain well, then transfer to a large bowl.

4 While the potatoes are still warm, pour over the Aïoli sauce and gently toss the potatoes in it. Adding the sauce to the potatoes while they are still warm will help them to absorb the garlic flavor. Let stand for 20 minutes so that the potatoes marinate in the sauce.

5 Transfer the potatoes with Aïoli to a warmed serving dish. Sprinkle over the parsley and salt to taste and serve warm. Alternatively, the dish can be prepared ahead and stored in the refrigerator, but return it to room temperature before serving.

Ham-wrapped Potatoes

SERVES FOUR

12 new potatoes, unpeeled

2 tbsp olive oil

12 slices serrano ham

salt

COOK'S TIP: Try to find potatoes that are all about the same size so that they cook evenly.

1 Preheat the oven to 400°F/200°C. Place the potatoes in a steamer set over a pan of boiling water. Cover and steam for 30 minutes, or until tender. Remove from the heat and let cool slightly.

2 Pour the olive oil into an ovenproof dish. Wrap each potato in a slice of ham and arrange in the dish in a single layer. Roast in the preheated oven, turning occasionally, for 20 minutes.

3 Transfer the potatoes to warmed serving dishes. Season to taste with salt and serve immediately or let cool a little before serving.

Feisty Potatoes

SERVES SIX

1 x quantity Fried Potatoes
   (see page 7)
1 x quantity Aïoli (see page 12)

CHILI OIL

⅔ cup olive oil
2 small hot fresh red chilies,
   slit
1 tsp hot Spanish paprika

COOK'S TIP: You will find
as many "authentic" recipes
for this dish as there are
cooks in Spain: sometimes the
potatoes are deep-fried, and
often the aïoli and chili oil
are mixed together.

1 To make the chili oil, heat the olive oil and chilies over high heat until the chilies begin to sizzle. Remove the pan from the heat and stir in the paprika. Set aside and let cool, then transfer the chili oil to a pourer with a spout. Do not strain.

2 Cook the potatoes, and while they cook make the Aïoli.

3 To serve, divide the potatoes between 6 serving plates and add a dollop of Aïoli to each. Drizzle with chili oil and serve warm or at room temperature. In Spain these are served with wooden toothpicks.

Peppered Potatoes

SERVES SIX-EIGHT

2 lb/900 g new potatoes,
  unpeeled
½ cup olive oil
1 tbsp sherry vinegar
1 tbsp sun-dried tomato
  paste
1 tsp paprika
pinch of cayenne pepper
salt

1 Place the potatoes in a large pan of lightly salted water and bring to a boil. Reduce the heat, then cover and let simmer for 15–20 minutes, or until just tender. Drain and let cool.

2 Meanwhile, make the sauce. Mix 5 tablespoons of the olive oil, the vinegar, tomato paste, paprika, and cayenne pepper together in a large bowl and season to taste with salt. Reserve until required.

3 Heat the remaining olive oil in a large, heavy-bottom skillet. Cut the potatoes into fourths and add to the skillet, in batches if necessary. Cook over medium heat, stirring and turning occasionally, for 8–10 minutes, or until crisp and golden brown. Drain with a slotted spoon and add to the bowl containing the sauce.

4 When all the potatoes have been cooked, toss gently in the sauce, then divide between warmed serving dishes. Serve immediately.

Fried Potatoes with Piquant Paprika

SERVES SIX

3 tsp paprika
1 tsp ground cumin
¼–½ tsp cayenne pepper
½ tsp salt
1 lb/450 g small old potatoes,
   peeled
corn oil, for shallow-frying
fresh parsley sprigs,
   to garnish
Aïoli (see page 12),
   to serve (optional)

VARIATION: Cook the potatoes as here, then spoon over the Fiery Tomato Salsa that accompanies the Cheese Puffs (see page 112), or serve the salsa separately for dipping the potatoes in. This dish is then known as Patatas Bravas (Bold Potatoes).

1 Place the paprika, ground cumin, cayenne pepper, and salt in a small bowl and mix well together. Reserve.

2 Cut each potato into 8 thick wedges. Pour enough corn oil into a large, heavy-bottom skillet so that it comes about 1 inch/2.5 cm up the sides of the skillet. Heat the oil, then add the potato wedges, preferably in a single layer, and

cook gently for 10 minutes, or until golden brown all over, turning occasionally. Remove from the skillet with a slotted spoon and drain on paper towels.

3 Transfer the potato wedges to a large bowl and, while they are still hot, sprinkle with the paprika mixture, then gently toss them together to coat.

4 Turn the fried potatoes with paprika into one large, warmed serving dish, several smaller ones, or individual serving plates and serve hot, garnished with parsley sprigs. Accompany with a bowl of Aïoli for dipping, if wished.

Warm Potato Salad

SERVES FOUR-SIX

¾ cup olive oil

1 lb/450 g waxy potatoes, thinly sliced

¼ cup white wine vinegar

2 garlic cloves, finely chopped

salt and pepper

COOK'S TIP: To serve this salad with a platter of mixed tapas, either combine with other warm dishes or let it cool completely before serving.

1 Heat ¼ cup of the olive oil in a large, heavy-bottom skillet. Add the potato slices and season to taste with salt, then cook over low heat, shaking the skillet occasionally, for 10 minutes. Turn the potatoes over and cook for an additional 5 minutes, or until tender but not browned.

2 Meanwhile, pour the vinegar into a small pan. Add the garlic and season to taste with pepper. Bring to a boil, then stir in the remaining olive oil.

3 Transfer the potatoes to a bowl and pour over the dressing. Toss gently and let stand for 15 minutes. Using a slotted spoon, transfer the potatoes to individual serving dishes and serve warm.

Russian Salad

SERVES SIX

2 eggs

1 lb/450 g baby new
  potatoes, cut into fourths

4 oz/115 g fine green beans,
  cut into 1-inch/2.5-cm
  lengths

4 oz/115 g frozen peas

4 oz/115 g carrots

7 oz/200 g canned tuna in
  olive oil, drained

8 tbsp mayonnaise

2 tbsp lemon juice

1 garlic clove, crushed

4 small gherkins, sliced

8 pitted black olives, halved

1 tbsp capers

1 tbsp chopped fresh
  flatleaf parsley

1 tbsp chopped fresh dill, plus
  extra sprigs to garnish

salt and pepper

1 Place the eggs in a pan, then cover with cold water and slowly bring to a boil. Immediately reduce the heat to very low, then cover and simmer gently for 10 minutes. As soon as the eggs are cooked, drain them and place under cold running water until they are cold. By doing this quickly, you will prevent a black ring forming around the egg yolk. Gently tap the eggs to crack the eggshells and let stand until cold.

2 Meanwhile, place the potatoes in a large pan of cold, salted water and bring to a boil. Reduce the heat and simmer for 7 minutes, or until just tender. Add the beans and peas to the pan for the last 2 minutes of cooking. Drain well and splash under cold running water, then let the vegetables cool completely.

3 Cut the carrots into julienne strips about 1 inch/2.5 cm in length. Flake the tuna into large chunks. When the potatoes, beans, and peas are cold, place them in a large bowl. Add the carrot strips and the flaked tuna and very gently toss the ingredients together. Transfer the vegetables and tuna to a large salad bowl or serving dish.

4 Place the mayonnaise in a pitcher, then stir in the lemon juice to thin it slightly. Stir in the garlic and season to taste with salt and pepper. Drizzle the mayonnaise dressing over the vegetables and tuna.

5 Sprinkle the gherkins, olives and capers into the salad and finally sprinkle over the parsley and dill. You can store the salad in the refrigerator but return to room temperature before serving. Just before serving, shell the eggs and slice into wedges. Add the eggs to the salad, then garnish with dill sprigs and serve.

Potato Wedges with Roasted Garlic Dip

SERVES EIGHT

3 lb/1.3 kg potatoes, unpeeled
  and halved
2 tbsp olive oil
1 garlic clove, finely chopped
2 tsp salt

ROASTED GARLIC DIP

2 garlic bulbs, separated
  into cloves
1 tbsp olive oil
5 tbsp sour cream or
  strained plain yogurt
4 tbsp mayonnaise
paprika, to taste
salt

1 First, make the roasted garlic dip. Preheat the oven to 400°F/ 200°C. Place the garlic cloves in an ovenproof dish, then pour in the olive oil and toss to coat. Spread out in a single layer and roast in the preheated oven for 25 minutes, or until tender. Remove from the oven and let stand until cool enough to handle.

2 Peel the garlic cloves, then place on a heavy cutting board and sprinkle with a little salt. Mash well with a fork until smooth. Scrape into a bowl and stir in the sour cream and mayonnaise. Season to taste with salt and paprika. Cover the bowl with plastic wrap and let chill until ready to serve.

3 To cook the potatoes, cut each potato half into 3 wedges and place in a large bowl. Add the olive oil, garlic, and salt and toss well. Transfer the wedges to a roasting pan, then arrange in a single layer and roast in the preheated oven for 1–1¼ hours, or until crisp and golden.

4 Remove from the oven and transfer to serving bowls. Serve immediately, handing round the roasted garlic dip separately.

VARIATION: You can also serve the potato wedges with Aïoli (see page 12) or simply with good-quality mayonnaise, if you are in a hurry.

"Wrinkled" Potatoes with Mojo Sauce

SERVES FOUR-SIX

3½ tbsp sea salt

24 small, new red-skinned
potatoes, unpeeled and
kept whole

MOJO SAUCE

1½ oz/40 g day-old bread,
crusts removed and torn
into small pieces

2 large garlic cloves

½ tsp salt

1½ tbsp hot Spanish paprika

1 tbsp ground cumin

about 2 tbsp red wine
vinegar

about 5 tbsp extra-virgin
olive oil

2 pimientos del piquillo
(see page 160), drained

1 Pour about 1 inch/2.5 cm water into a pan and stir in the sea salt. Add the potatoes and stir again. They do not have to be covered with water. Fold a clean dish towel to fit over the potatoes, then bring the water to a boil. Reduce the heat and let simmer for 20 minutes, or until the potatoes are tender, but still holding together.

2 Remove the dish towel and reserve. Drain the potatoes and return them to the empty pan. When the dish towel is cool enough to handle, wring the saltwater it contains into the pan. Place the pan over low heat and

shake until the potatoes are dry and coated with a thin white film. Remove from the heat.

3 Meanwhile, make the Mojo Sauce. Place the bread in a bowl and add just enough water to cover. Let stand for 5 minutes to soften. Use your hands to squeeze all the water from the bread. Use a pestle and mortar to mash the garlic and salt into a paste. Stir in the paprika and cumin. Transfer the mixture to a food processor. Add 2 tablespoons of vinegar and blend. Add the bread and 2 tablespoons of olive oil and blend again.

4 With the motor still running, add the pimientos one at a time and blend until puréed and a sauce forms. Add more olive oil, if necessary, until the sauce is smooth and thick. Taste and adjust the seasoning, adding extra vinegar, if necessary.

5 To serve, cut the potatoes in half and spear with toothpicks. Serve hot or at room temperature with a bowl of sauce on the side for dipping.

Eggplant Dip

SERVES SIX–EIGHT

1 large eggplant, about
   14 oz/400 g
5 tbsp olive oil
2 scallions, finely chopped
1 large garlic clove, crushed
2 tbsp finely chopped fresh
   parsley
salt and pepper
smoked sweet Spanish
   paprika, to garnish
French bread, to serve

1 Cut the eggplant into thick slices and sprinkle with salt to draw out any bitterness. Let stand for 30 minutes, then rinse and pat dry.

2 Heat 4 tablespoons of the olive oil in a large skillet over medium–high heat. Add the eggplant slices and cook on both sides until soft and beginning to brown. Remove from the skillet and let cool. The slices will release the oil again as they cool.

3 Heat the remaining olive oil in the skillet. Add the scallions and garlic and cook for 3 minutes, or until the scallions become soft. Remove from the heat and reserve with the eggplant slices to cool.

4 Transfer all the ingredients to a food processor and process just until a coarse purée forms. Transfer to a serving bowl and stir in the parsley. Taste and adjust the seasoning, if necessary. Serve immediately, or cover and let chill until 15 minutes before required. Sprinkle with paprika and serve with French bread.

Eggplant & Bell Pepper Dip

SERVES SIX–EIGHT

2 large eggplants

2 red bell peppers

4 tbsp Spanish olive oil

2 garlic cloves, coarsely
 chopped

grated rind and juice of
 ½ lemon

1 tbsp chopped cilantro, plus
 extra sprigs to garnish

½–1 tsp paprika

salt and pepper

bread or toast, to serve

1 Preheat the oven to 375°F/190°C. Prick the skins of the eggplants and bell peppers all over with a fork and brush with 1 tablespoon of the olive oil. Place on a baking sheet and bake in the preheated oven for 45 minutes, or until the skins are beginning to turn black, the flesh of the eggplant is very soft, and the bell peppers are deflated.

2 Place the cooked vegetables in a bowl and cover tightly with a clean, damp dish towel. Alternatively, place the vegetables in a plastic bag and let stand for about 15 minutes, or until cool enough to handle.

3 When the vegetables have cooled, cut the eggplants in half lengthwise, carefully scoop out

the flesh and discard the skin. Cut the eggplant flesh into large chunks. Remove and discard the stem, core, and seeds from the bell peppers and cut the flesh into large pieces.

4 Heat the remaining olive oil in a skillet. Add the eggplant and bell pepper and cook for 5 minutes. Add the garlic and cook for 30 seconds.

5 Turn the contents of the skillet onto paper towels to drain, then transfer to a food processor. Add the lemon rind and juice, the chopped cilantro, the paprika, and salt and pepper to taste, then process until a speckled purée is formed.

6 Transfer the eggplant and bell pepper dip to a serving bowl. Serve warm, at room temperature, or let cool for 30 minutes, then let chill in the refrigerator for at least 1 hour, then serve cold. Garnish with cilantro sprigs and accompany with thick slices of bread or toast for dipping.

VARIATION: Instead of cooking the eggplants and bell peppers in the oven, they can be cooked under a preheated broiler until the skins are charred all over. They do, however, need to be turned frequently and will take about 10 minutes. This dip is also very good served with cold meats.

Marinated Eggplants

SERVES FOUR

2 eggplants, halved lengthwise

4 tbsp olive oil

2 garlic cloves, finely chopped

2 tbsp chopped fresh parsley

1 tbsp chopped fresh thyme

2 tbsp lemon juice

salt and pepper

COOK'S TIP: Modern varieties of eggplant are less bitter, so there is no need to salt them, especially if they are to be roasted rather than fried.

1 Make 2–3 slashes in the flesh of the eggplant halves and place, cut-side down, in an ovenproof dish. Season to taste with salt and pepper, then pour over the olive oil and sprinkle with the garlic, parsley, and thyme. Cover and let marinate at room temperature for 2–3 hours.

2 Preheat the oven to 350°F/180°C. Uncover the dish and roast the eggplants in the preheated oven for 45 minutes. Remove the dish from the oven and turn the eggplants over. Baste with the cooking juices and sprinkle with the lemon juice. Return to the oven and cook for an additional 15 minutes.

3 Transfer the eggplants to serving plates. Spoon over the cooking juices and serve hot or warm.

Sweet Onion Salad

SERVES FOUR-SIX

4 Spanish onions
2 tbsp chopped fresh parsley
⅔ cup black olives, pitted
1 tbsp sherry vinegar
2 tbsp red wine vinegar
½ cup olive oil
about 1 tbsp water
salt and pepper

COOK'S TIP: Spanish onions are both large and mild. If you are unable to find them, substitute red or white onions, which are also sweet. They tend to be smaller, so you may need 5 or 6.

1 Bring a large pan of lightly salted water to a boil. Add the onions and simmer for 20 minutes, or until tender. Drain and let stand until cool enough to handle.

2 Thickly slice the onions and place in a shallow dish. Sprinkle over the parsley and olives and season to taste with pepper.

3 Whisk the vinegars and olive oil together in a bowl, then whisk in enough of the water to make a creamy vinaigrette.

4 Pour the dressing over the onions and serve at room temperature.

Baked Stuffed Onions

SERVES FOUR

4 large Spanish onions
2 slices lean bacon, diced
1/2 red bell pepper, halved,
    deseeded, and diced
generous 1 cup fresh ground
    lean beef
1 tbsp chopped mixed fresh
    herbs, such as parsley,
    rosemary, and thyme or
    1 tsp dried mixed herbs
butter, for greasing
1 1/4 cups beef stock
1/2 cup fresh white bread
    crumbs
butter, for greasing
salt and pepper
cooked long-grain rice,
    garnished with chopped
    fresh parsley, to serve

GRAVY

1/4 stick butter
generous 2 cups finely
    chopped mushrooms
1 1/4 cups beef stock
2 tbsp cornstarch
2 tbsp water

1 Preheat the oven to 350°F/180°C. Place the onions in a pan of lightly salted water, then bring to a boil. Reduce the heat and let simmer for 15 minutes, or until tender.

2 Remove the onions from the pan, then drain and cool slightly. Hollow out the centers and finely chop the inner flesh.

3 Heat a skillet and cook the bacon until the fat runs out. Add the chopped onion and red bell pepper and cook for 5–7 minutes, stirring frequently.

4 Add the beef to the skillet and cook, stirring, for 3 minutes, or until browned. Remove the skillet from the heat and stir in the herbs and bread crumbs. Season to taste with salt and pepper.

5 Grease an ovenproof dish and stand the whole onions in it. Pack the beef mixture into the centers and pour the stock around them. Bake the onions in the preheated oven for 1–1¹/2 hours, or until tender.

6 To make the gravy, heat the butter in a small pan. Add the mushrooms and cook for 3–4 minutes. Strain the liquid from the onions and add to the pan with the stock, then cook for 2–3 minutes.

7 Mix the cornstarch with the water, then stir into the gravy and heat, stirring, until thickened and smooth. Season to taste with salt and pepper. Serve the onions with the gravy and rice, garnished with parsley.

Moorish Fava Bean Dip

SERVES SIX

1 lb 2 oz/500 g shelled fresh
  or frozen fava beans
5 tbsp olive oil
1 garlic clove, finely chopped
1 onion, finely chopped
1 tsp ground cumin
1 tbsp lemon juice
3/4 cup water
1 tbsp chopped fresh mint
salt and pepper
paprika, to garnish
raw vegetables, crusty bread
  or breadsticks, to serve

1 If using fresh fava beans, bring a large pan of lightly salted water to a boil. Add the beans, then reduce the heat and simmer, covered, for 7 minutes. Drain well, then refresh under cold running water and drain again. Remove and discard the outer skins. If using frozen beans, let thaw completely, then remove and discard the outer skins.

2 Heat 1 tablespoon of the olive oil in a skillet. Add the garlic, onion, and cumin and cook over low heat, stirring occasionally, until the onion is softened and translucent. Add the fava beans and cook, stirring frequently, for 5 minutes.

3 Remove the skillet from the heat and transfer the mixture to a food processor or blender. Add the lemon juice, the remaining olive oil, water, and mint and process to a paste. Season to taste with salt and pepper.

4 Scrape the paste back into the skillet and heat gently until warm. Transfer to individual serving bowls and dust lightly with paprika. Serve with dippers of your choice.

COOK'S TIP: Classic Arab spices and herbs still feature in modern Spanish cuisine, especially in the south of the country.

Fava Beans with Cheese & Shrimp

SERVES SIX

1 lb 2 oz/500 g shelled fresh
   or frozen fava beans
2 fresh thyme sprigs
8 oz/225 g cooked shelled
   shrimp
8 oz/225 g Queso Majorero
   or Gruyère cheese, diced
6 tbsp olive oil
2 tbsp lemon juice
1 garlic clove, finely chopped
salt and pepper

1 Bring a large pan of lightly salted water to a boil. Add the fava beans and 1 thyme sprig, then reduce the heat and simmer, covered, for 7 minutes. Drain well and refresh under cold running water, then drain again.

2 Unless the fava beans are very young, remove and discard the outer skins. Place the

beans in a bowl and add the shrimp and cheese.

3 Chop the remaining thyme sprig. Whisk the olive oil, lemon juice, garlic, and chopped thyme together in a separate bowl and season to taste with salt and pepper.

4 Pour the dressing over the bean mixture. Toss lightly and serve.

Fava Beans with Serrano Ham

SERVES SIX-EIGHT

2 oz/55 g serrano ham,
   prosciutto, pancetta, or
   rindless smoked lean bacon
4 oz/115 g chorizo sausage,
   outer casing removed
4 tbsp Spanish olive oil
1 onion, finely chopped
2 garlic cloves, finely chopped
splash of dry white wine
1 lb/450 g frozen fava beans,
   thawed, or about 3 lb/1.3 kg
   fresh fava beans in their
   pods, shelled to give
   1 lb/450 g
1 tbsp chopped fresh dill or
   mint, plus extra to garnish
pinch of sugar
salt and pepper

1 Cut the ham, pancetta, or bacon into small strips. Cut the chorizo into 3/4-inch/2-cm cubes. Heat the oil in a heavy-bottom skillet or flameproof dish with a lid. Add the onion and cook for 5 minutes, or until softened. If using pancetta or bacon, add it with the onion. Add the garlic and cook for an additional 30 seconds.

2 Pour the wine into the skillet, then increase the heat and let it bubble to evaporate the alcohol, then reduce the heat. Add the fava beans, ham, if using, and the chorizo and cook for 1–2 minutes, stirring all the time to coat in the oil.

3 Cover the skillet and let the beans simmer gently in the oil, stirring occasionally, for 10–15 minutes, or until the beans are tender. You may need to add water to the skillet during cooking, so keep an eye on it and add a splash if the beans become too dry. Stir in the dill and sugar. Season to taste with salt and pepper, but taste first as it may not need any salt.

4 Transfer the fava beans to a large, warmed serving dish, several smaller ones, or individual plates and serve piping hot, garnished with chopped dill.

Mixed Beans

SERVES FOUR-SIX

6 oz/175 g shelled fresh or
   frozen fava beans
4 oz/115 g fresh or frozen
   green beans
4 oz/115 g snow peas
1 shallot, finely chopped
6 fresh mint sprigs
4 tbsp olive oil
1 tbsp sherry vinegar
1 garlic clove, finely chopped
salt and pepper

1 Bring a large pan of lightly salted water to a boil. Add the fava beans and reduce the heat, then cover and simmer for 7 minutes. Remove the beans with a slotted spoon, then plunge into cold water and drain. Remove and discard the outer skins.

2 Meanwhile, return the pan of salted water to a boil. Add the green beans and return to a boil again. Drain and refresh under cold running water. Drain well.

3 Mix the fava beans, green beans, snow peas, and shallot together in a bowl. Strip the leaves from the mint sprigs, then reserve half and add the remainder to the bean mixture. Finely chop the reserved mint.

4 Whisk the olive oil, vinegar, garlic, and chopped mint together in a separate bowl and season to taste with salt and pepper. Pour the dressing over the bean mixture and toss lightly to coat. Cover with plastic wrap and let chill until required.

Stuffed Cherry Tomatoes

SERVES EIGHT

24 cherry tomatoes

ANCHOVY & OLIVE FILLING

1¾ oz/50 g canned anchovy
   fillets in olive oil

8 pimiento-stuffed green
   olives, finely chopped

2 large hard-cooked eggs,
   finely chopped

pepper

CRAB MAYONNAISE FILLING

6 oz/175 g canned crabmeat,
   drained

4 tbsp mayonnaise

1 tbsp chopped fresh flatleaf
   parsley

salt and pepper

paprika, to garnish

BLACK OLIVE & CAPER FILLING

12 pitted black olives

3 tbsp capers

6 tbsp Aïoli (see page 12)

salt and pepper

1 If necessary, cut and discard a very thin slice from the stem end of each tomato to make the bases flat and stable. Cut a thin slice from the smooth end of each cherry tomato and discard. Using a serrated knife or teaspoon, loosen the pulp and seeds of each and scoop out, discarding the flesh. Turn the scooped-out tomatoes upside down on paper towels and let drain for 5 minutes.

2 To make the anchovy and olive filling, drain the anchovies, reserving the olive oil for later, then chop finely and place in a bowl. Add the olives and hard-cooked eggs. Pour in a trickle of the reserved olive oil to moisten the mixture, then season with pepper. (Don't add salt to season, as the anchovies are salty.) Mix well together.

3 To make the crab mayonnaise filling, place the crabmeat, mayonnaise and parsley in a bowl and mix well together. Season the filling to taste with salt and pepper. Sprinkle with paprika before serving.

4 To make the black olive and caper filling, place the olives and capers on paper towels to drain them well, then chop finely and place in a bowl. Add the Aïoli and mix well together. Season the filling to taste with salt and pepper.

5 Fill a pastry bag fitted with a 3/4-inch/2-cm plain tip with the filling of your choice and use to fill the hollow tomato shells. Store the cherry tomatoes in the refrigerator until ready to serve.

Tomato & Olive Salad

SERVES SIX

2 tbsp sherry or red wine vinegar

5 tbsp olive oil

1 garlic clove, finely chopped

1 tsp paprika

4 tomatoes, peeled and diced

12 anchovy-stuffed or pimiento-stuffed olives

½ cucumber, peeled and diced

2 shallots, finely chopped

1 tbsp pickled capers in brine, drained

2–3 chicory heads, separated into leaves

salt

1 First, make the dressing. Whisk the vinegar, olive oil, garlic, and paprika together in a bowl. Season to taste with salt and reserve.

2 Place the tomatoes, olives, cucumber, shallots, and capers in a separate bowl. Pour over the dressing and toss lightly.

3 Line 6 individual serving bowls with chicory leaves. Spoon an equal quantity of the salad into the center of each and serve.

Stuffed Tomatoes with Rice

SERVES FOUR–EIGHT

3/4 cup long-grain rice

generous 3/4 cup black olives,
    pitted and chopped

3 tbsp olive oil

4 beefsteak or other large
    tomatoes, halved

4 tbsp chopped fresh parsley

salt and pepper

1 Bring a large pan of lightly salted water to a boil. Add the rice, then return to a boil and stir once. Reduce the heat and cook for 10–15 minutes, or until only just tender. Drain well, then rinse under cold running water and drain again. Line a large, shallow dish with paper towels and spread out the rice on top for about 1 hour to dry.

2 Mix the rice, olives, and olive oil together in a bowl and season well with pepper. You will probably not require any additional salt. Cover with plastic wrap and let stand at room temperature for 8 hours or overnight.

3 Cut a slice off the tops of the tomatoes and, using a teaspoon, carefully scoop out and discard the seeds without piercing the shells. Scoop out the flesh, then finely chop and add to the rice and olive mixture. Season the insides of the shells to taste with salt, then turn them upside down on paper towels and let drain for 1 hour.

4 Pat the insides of the tomato shells dry with paper towels, then divide the rice and olive mixture between them. Sprinkle with the parsley and serve.

VARIATION: This filling is also delicious in red or yellow bell peppers. Halve and seed the bell peppers, then blanch in lightly salted boiling water for 5 minutes. Drain well and refresh under cold running water, then drain again. Peel and seed 4 standard tomatoes and add the chopped flesh to the rice and olive mixture.

Garlic Tomatoes

SERVES SIX

8 deep red tomatoes
3 fresh thyme sprigs, plus
    extra to garnish
12 garlic cloves, unpeeled
generous ¼ cup olive oil
salt and pepper

COOK'S TIP: Sun-ripened tomatoes are perfect for this dish as they have a much fuller, sweeter flavor than tomatoes ripened under glass.

1 Preheat the oven to 425°F/220°C. Cut the tomatoes in half lengthwise and arrange, cut-side up, in a single layer in a large, ovenproof dish. Tuck the thyme sprigs and garlic cloves between them.

2 Drizzle the olive oil all over the tomatoes and season to taste with pepper. Bake in the preheated oven for 40–45 minutes, or until the tomatoes are softened and beginning to char slightly around the edges.

3 Remove and discard the thyme sprigs. Season the tomatoes to taste with salt and pepper. Garnish with the extra thyme sprigs and serve hot or warm. Squeeze the pulp from the garlic over the tomatoes at the table.

Zucchini with Cheese & Vinaigrette

SERVES SIX

1 lb 4 oz/550 g zucchini,
  sliced lengthwise

6 tbsp olive oil

6 oz/175 g young Manchego
  or mozzarella cheese,
  diced

salt and pepper

fresh lemon balm leaves,
  to garnish

LEMON VINAIGRETTE

5 tbsp olive oil

4 tbsp lemon juice

1 tbsp clear honey

1 tsp finely grated lemon rind

1 Preheat the oven to 400°F/200°C. Place the zucchini in a roasting pan, then pour over the olive oil and season to taste with salt and pepper. Toss well to coat. Roast in the preheated oven, stirring and tossing 2–3 times, for 30 minutes, or until golden brown.

2 Meanwhile, make the lemon vinaigrette. Whisk the olive oil, lemon juice, honey, and lemon rind together in a bowl and season to taste with salt and pepper.

3 Transfer the zucchini to a serving dish and pour over the vinaigrette. Toss gently and let cool to room temperature. Just before serving, sprinkle over the cheese and garnish with lemon balm leaves.

Zucchini Fritters with a Dipping Sauce

SERVES SIX-EIGHT

1 lb/450 g baby zucchini
3 tbsp all-purpose flour
1 tsp paprika
1 large egg
2 tbsp milk
corn oil, for shallow-frying
coarse sea salt
dipping sauce such as
Aïoli (see page 12), Fiery
   Tomato Salsa (see page
   112), or the Pine Nut
   Sauce (see below)

PINE NUT SAUCE

scant ⅔ cup pine nuts
1 garlic clove, peeled
3 tbsp Spanish extra-virgin
   olive oil
1 tbsp lemon juice
3 tbsp water
1 tbsp chopped fresh
   flatleaf parsley
salt and pepper

1 If you have chosen to serve the Pine Nut Sauce with the zucchini fritters, then make this first. Place the pine nuts and garlic in a food processor and process to form a purée. With the motor still running, gradually add the olive oil, lemon juice, and water to form a smooth sauce. Stir in the parsley and season to taste with salt and pepper. Transfer to a serving bowl and reserve until required.

2 To prepare the zucchini, cut them on the diagonal into thin slices about $^{1}/_{4}$ inch/5 mm thick. Place the flour and paprika in a plastic bag and mix together. Beat the egg and milk together in a large bowl.

3 Add the zucchini slices to the flour mixture and toss well together until coated. Shake off the excess flour. Heat the corn oil in a large, heavy-bottom skillet to a depth of about $^{1}/_{2}$ inch/1 cm. Dip the zucchini slices, one at a time, into the egg mixture, then slip them into the hot oil. Cook the zucchini slices in batches in a single layer so that they do not overcrowd the skillet, for 2 minutes, or until they are crisp and golden brown.

4 Using a slotted spoon, remove the zucchini fritters from the skillet and drain on paper towels. Continue until all the zucchini slices have been fried.

5 Serve the zucchini fritters piping hot, lightly sprinkled with sea salt. Accompany with a bowl of your chosen dipping sauce.

VARIATION: Eggplants can be cooked in the same way, while the Pine Nut Sauce can be made with almonds, if you prefer.

Deep-Fried Green Chilies

EACH 9-OZ/250-G BAG OF
CHILIES SERVES FOUR-SIX

olive oil
sweet or hot fresh green
  chilies
sea salt

VARIATION: For a more
elaborate tapas, top a thin
slice of bread with a fried
egg, yolk-side up. Secure the
egg to the bread by skewering
the set white to the bread
with a wooden toothpick with
a fried chili or pimiento de
Padrón on it.

1 Heat 3 inches/7.5 cm of olive oil in a large, heavy-bottom pan until it reaches 375°F/190°C, or until a cube of bread turns brown in 30 seconds.

2 Rinse the chilies and pat them very dry with paper towels. Drop them in the hot oil for no longer than 20 seconds, or until they turn bright green and the skins blister.

3 Remove with a slotted spoon and drain well on crumpled paper towels. Sprinkle with sea salt and serve immediately.

Deep-Fried Cauliflower

SERVES FOUR-SIX

1 cauliflower, cut into florets

1 egg

2/3 cup milk

generous 3/4 cup all-purpose flour

vegetable oil, for deep-frying

salt

Tomato & Bell Pepper Salsa (see page 7), or Aïoli (see page 12), to serve

COOK'S TIP: Fritters of every sort feature in traditional tapas bars throughout Spain. They may be served on their own or with a tasty sauce for dipping.

1 Bring a large pan of lightly salted water to a boil. Add the cauliflower florets, then reduce the heat and simmer gently for 5 minutes. Drain well, then refresh under cold running water and drain again.

2 Beat the egg and milk together in a bowl until combined. Gradually whisk in the flour and 1 teaspoon salt.

3 Meanwhile, heat the vegetable oil for deep-frying to 350°–375°F/ 180°–190°C, or until a cube of bread browns in 30 seconds.

4 Dip the cauliflower florets in the batter and drain off the excess, then deep-fry, in batches if necessary, for 5 minutes, or until golden. Drain on paper towels, then serve immediately in warmed bowls with Tomato & Bell Pepper Salsa or Aïoli.

Green Beans with Pine Nuts

SERVES EIGHT

2 tbsp Spanish olive oil
1/3 cup pine nuts
1/2–1 tsp paprika
1 lb/450 g green beans
1 small onion, finely chopped
1 garlic clove, finely chopped
juice of 1/2 lemon
salt and pepper

1 Heat the olive oil in a large, heavy-bottom skillet. Add the pine nuts and cook for 1 minute, stirring constantly and shaking the skillet, until light golden brown. Using a slotted spoon, remove the pine nuts from the skillet and drain well on paper towels, then transfer to a bowl. Reserve the oil in the skillet for later. Add the paprika, according to taste, to the pine nuts and stir together until coated, then reserve.

2 Trim the green beans and remove any strings if necessary. Place the beans in a pan, then pour over boiling water. Return to a boil and cook for 5 minutes, or until tender but still firm. Drain well in a colander.

3 Reheat the oil in the skillet. Add the onion and cook for 5–10 minutes, or until softened and beginning to brown. Add the garlic and fry for an additional 30 seconds.

4 Add the beans to the skillet and cook for 2–3 minutes, tossing together with the onion until heated through. Season to taste with salt and pepper.

5 Turn the contents of the skillet into a warmed serving dish. Sprinkle over the lemon juice and toss together. Sprinkle over the reserved golden pine nuts and serve hot.

Green Beans with Almonds

SERVES FOUR-SIX

1 lb 2 oz/500 g green beans
½ stick butter
1 oz/25 g slivered almonds
2 tsp lemon juice
salt

VARIATION: For a delicious variation to this dish, try substituting chopped, unsalted pistachio nuts for the almonds, and orange juice for the lemon juice.

1 Bring a pan of lightly salted water to a boil. Add the beans and let simmer for 8–10 minutes, or until just tender but still retaining a slight "bite."

2 Meanwhile, melt the butter in a heavy-bottom skillet. Add the almonds and cook over low heat, stirring frequently, for 3–5 minutes, or until golden. Stir in the lemon juice and season to taste with salt.

3 Drain the beans and add to the skillet. Stir well to mix, then transfer to individual serving dishes and serve warm.

Green Beans in Tomato Sauce

SERVES SIX
1/4 stick butter
2 garlic cloves, finely chopped
2 scallions, finely chopped
2 lb 4 oz/1 kg green beans, cut into 1-inch/2.5-cm lengths
1 lb 9 oz/700 g canned chopped tomatoes
1 tbsp pine nuts
1 tbsp lemon juice
1 bay leaf
salt and pepper

VARIATION: This is also a delicious way to serve snow peas—there is no need to cut them into shorter lengths.

1 Melt the butter in a large, heavy-bottom skillet. Add the garlic and scallions and cook over medium heat, stirring occasionally, for 3–4 minutes. Add the beans and cook, stirring frequently, for an additional 4 minutes.

2 Add the tomatoes with their can juices, pine nuts, lemon juice, and bay leaf and season to taste with salt and pepper. Reduce the heat and let simmer gently for 30 minutes, or until the beans are tender and the sauce is pulpy.

3 Remove and discard the bay leaf. Taste and adjust the seasoning if necessary. Transfer to warmed serving dishes and serve hot.

Buttered Cucumber

SERVES FOUR

1 large cucumber, peeled
  and halved lengthwise

½ stick butter

1 tbsp lemon juice

1 tbsp finely chopped
  fresh mint

salt and pepper

COOK'S TIP: You can serve this tapas with forks or with wooden toothpicks, depending on how dextrous your guests are.

1 Scoop out the seeds from the cucumber using a teaspoon. Cut each cucumber half into 3/4-inch/2-cm slices and place in a colander, sprinkling each layer with salt. Let drain for 30 minutes, then rinse under cold running water and drain well. Pat dry with paper towels.

2 Melt the butter in a large, heavy-bottom skillet. Add the cucumber and cook over medium heat, stirring constantly, for 3–5 minutes, or until thoroughly hot.

3 Stir in the lemon juice and mint and season to taste with pepper. Transfer to warmed serving dishes and serve hot.

Moorish Zucchini Salad

SERVES FOUR-SIX

1lb 2 oz/500 g small zucchini
about 4 tbsp olive oil
1 large garlic clove, halved
1/3 cup pine nuts
1/3 cup raisins
3 tbsp finely chopped fresh
    mint leaves (not spearmint
    or peppermint)
about 2 tbsp lemon juice, or
    to taste
salt and pepper

1 Slice the zucchini thinly. Heat the oil in a large skillet over medium heat. Add the garlic and let it cook until golden to flavor the oil, then remove and discard. Add the zucchini and cook, stirring, until just tender. Immediately remove from the skillet and transfer to a large serving bowl.

2 Add the pine nuts, raisins, mint, lemon juice, and salt and pepper to taste, and stir. Taste, and add more olive oil, lemon juice, and seasoning, if necessary.

3 Let the salad cool completely. Cover and chill for at least 3^1/2 hours. Remove from the refrigerator 10 minutes before serving.

COOK'S TIP: This salad is best made with young, tender zucchini no more than 1 inch/2.5 cm thick. If using older, larger zucchini, cut them in half or fourths lengthwise first, then slice thinly.

VARIATION: For a more robust flavor, chop 4 drained anchovy fillets in oil and add in Step 2.

Orange & Fennel Salad

SERVES FOUR

4 large, juicy oranges

1 large fennel bulb, very
  thinly sliced

1 mild white onion, finely
  sliced

2 tbsp extra-virgin olive oil

12 plump black olives, pitted
  and thinly sliced

1 fresh red chili, deseeded
  and very thinly sliced
  (optional)

finely chopped fresh parsley

French bread, to serve

1 Finely grate the rind from the oranges into a bowl and reserve. Using a small, serrated knife, remove all the white pith from the oranges, working over a bowl to catch the juices. Cut the oranges horizontally into thin slices.

2 Toss the orange slices with the fennel and onion slices. Whisk the olive oil into the reserved orange juice, then spoon over the oranges. Sprinkle the olive slices over the top, add the chili, if using, then sprinkle with the orange rind and parsley. Serve with slices of French bread.

Pimientos with Curd Cheese & Fresh Herbs

MAKES SEVEN-EIGHT

6½ oz/185 g canned or
  bottled whole pimientos del
  piquillo
  (see page 160)
salt and pepper
fresh herb sprigs, to garnish

CURD CHEESE & HERB FILLING

8 oz/225 g curd cheese
1 tsp lemon juice
1 garlic clove, crushed
4 tbsp chopped fresh
  flatleaf parsley
1 tbsp chopped fresh mint
1 tbsp chopped fresh oregano

TUNA MAYONNAISE FILLING

7 oz/200 g canned tuna in
  olive oil, drained
5 tbsp mayonnaise
2 tsp lemon juice
2 tbsp chopped fresh
  flatleaf parsley

**GOAT CHEESE & OLIVE
FILLING**

1¾ oz/50 g pitted black
  olives, finely chopped
7 oz/200 g soft goat cheese
1 garlic clove, crushed

1 There is a choice of fillings provided in this recipe—the final decision is yours. Lift the sweet peppers from the jar, reserving the oil for later use.

2 To make the curd cheese and herb filling, place the curd cheese in a bowl and add the lemon juice, garlic, parsley, mint, and oregano. Mix well together. Season to taste with salt and pepper.

3 To make the tuna and mayonnaise filling, place the tuna in a bowl and add the

mayonnaise, lemon juice, and parsley. Add 1 tablespoon of the reserved oil from the jar of pimientos and mix well. Season to taste with salt and pepper.

4 To make the goat cheese and olive filling, place the olives in a bowl and add the goat cheese, garlic, and 1 tablespoon of

the reserved oil from the jar of pimientos. Mix well together. Season to taste with salt and pepper.

5 Using a teaspoon, heap the filling of your choice into each pimiento. Let chill in the refrigerator for at least 2 hours until firm.

6 To serve the pimientos, arrange them on a serving plate and, if necessary, wipe with paper towels to remove any of the filling that has spread over the skins. Garnish with herb sprigs and serve.

Asparagus & Fried Eggs

SERVES SIX

1 lb 2 oz/500 g asparagus
    spears
2 tbsp olive oil
6 eggs

1 Trim and discard the coarse, woody ends of the asparagus spears. Make sure all the stems are about the same length, then tie them together loosely with clean kitchen string. If you have an asparagus steamer, you don't need to tie the stems together—just place them in the basket.

2 Bring a tall pan of lightly salted water to a boil. Add the asparagus, making sure that the tips are protruding above the water, then reduce the heat and let simmer for 10–15 minutes, or until tender. Test by piercing a stem just above the water level with the point of a sharp knife.

3 Meanwhile, heat a little of the olive oil in a large, heavy-bottom skillet. Add 2 eggs, if there is enough room, and cook over medium–low heat, or until the whites are just set and the yolks are still runny. Transfer to warmed serving plates and cook the remaining eggs in the same way.

4 Drain the asparagus and divide the spears between the plates. Serve immediately.

COOK'S TIP: The asparagus spears are eaten with the fingers and dipped in the egg yolk. The egg white is not eaten.

VARIATION: You can also serve the asparagus with lightly boiled eggs for dipping in the same way

Roasted Asparagus with Serrano Ham

MAKES TWELVE
2 tbsp Spanish olive oil
6 slices serrano ham
12 asparagus spears
pepper
Aïoli (see page 12), to serve

1 Preheat the oven to 400°F/200°C. Place half the olive oil in a roasting pan that will hold the asparagus spears in a single layer and swirl it around so that it covers the base. Cut each slice of serrano ham in half lengthwise.

2 Trim and discard the coarse woody ends of the asparagus spears, then wrap a slice of ham around the stem end of each spear. Place the wrapped spears in the prepared roasting pan and lightly brush with the remaining olive oil. Season the asparagus with pepper.

3 Roast the asparagus spears in the preheated oven for

10 minutes, depending on the thickness of the asparagus, until tender but still firm. Do not overcook the asparagus spears, as it is important that they are still firm, so that you can pick them up with your fingers.

4 Serve the roasted asparagus piping hot, accompanied by a bowl of Aïoli for dipping.

Charbroiled Leeks

SERVES FOUR

8 baby leeks
2 tbsp olive oil, plus extra
  for brushing
2 tbsp white wine vinegar
2 tbsp snipped fresh chives
2 tbsp chopped fresh parsley
1 tsp Dijon mustard
salt and pepper
fresh parsley sprigs, to garnish

1 Trim the leeks and halve length-wise. Rinse well to remove any grit and pat dry with paper towels.

2 Heat a grill pan and brush with olive oil. Add the leeks and cook over medium–high heat, turning occasionally, for 5 minutes. Transfer to a shallow dish.

3 Meanwhile, whisk the olive oil, vinegar, chives, parsley, and mustard together in a bowl and season to taste with salt and pepper. Pour over the leeks, turning to coat. Cover with plastic wrap and let marinate at room temperature, turning occasionally, for 30 minutes.

4 Divide the leeks between individual serving plates, then garnish with parsley sprigs and serve.

Roasted Bell Peppers with Honey & Almonds

SERVES SIX

8 red bell peppers, cut into
   fourths and deseeded
4 tbsp olive oil
2 garlic cloves, thinly sliced
1 oz/25 g flaked almonds
2 tbsp clear honey
2 tbsp sherry vinegar
2 tbsp chopped fresh parsley
salt and pepper

1 Preheat the broiler to high. Place the bell peppers, skin-side up, in a single layer on a baking sheet. Cook under the hot broiler for 8–10 minutes, or until the skins have blistered and blackened. Using tongs, transfer to a plastic bag. Tie the top and let cool.

2 When the bell peppers are cool enough to handle, peel off the skin with your fingers or a knife and discard it. Chop the flesh into bite-size pieces and place in a bowl.

3 Heat the olive oil in a large, heavy-bottom skillet. Add the garlic and cook over low heat, stirring frequently, for 4 minutes, or until golden. Stir in the almonds, honey, and vinegar, then pour the mixture over the bell pepper pieces. Add the parsley and season to taste with salt and pepper, then toss well.

4 Let cool to room temperature before transferring to serving dishes. The bell peppers may also be covered and stored in the refrigerator, but should be returned to room temperature to serve.

Roasted Bell Pepper Salad

SERVES EIGHT

3 red bell peppers
3 yellow bell peppers
5 tbsp Spanish extra-virgin
    olive oil
2 tbsp dry sherry vinegar
    or lemon juice
2 garlic cloves, crushed
pinch of sugar
1 tbsp capers
8 small black Spanish olives
salt and pepper
2 tbsp chopped fresh
    marjoram, plus extra
    sprigs to garnish

1 Preheat the broiler. Place all the peppers on a wire rack or broiler pan and cook under the hot broiler for 10 minutes, or until their skins have blackened and blistered all over, turning them frequently.

2 Remove the roasted bell peppers from the heat, then place them in a bowl and immediately cover tightly with a clean, damp dish towel.

3 Alternatively, place the bell peppers in a plastic bag. You will find that the steam helps to soften the skins and makes it easier to remove them. Let the bell peppers stand for about 15 minutes, or until they are cool enough to handle.

4 Holding 1 bell pepper at a time over a clean bowl, use a sharp knife to make a small hole in the base and gently squeeze out the juices and reserve them. Still holding the bell pepper over the bowl, carefully peel off the skin with your fingers or a knife and discard it. Cut the bell peppers in half and remove the stem, core, and seeds, then cut each bell pepper into neat

thin strips. Arrange the pepper strips attractively on a serving dish.

5 Add the olive oil, sherry vinegar, garlic, sugar, and salt and pepper to taste to the reserved pepper juices. Whisk together until combined, then drizzle the dressing over the salad.

6 Sprinkle the capers, olives, and chopped marjoram over the salad, then garnish with marjoram sprigs and serve at room temperature.

Artichoke Hearts & Asparagus

SERVES FOUR-SIX

1 lb/450 g asparagus spears

14 oz/400 g canned artichoke hearts, drained and rinsed

2 tbsp freshly squeezed orange juice

½ tsp finely grated orange rind

2 tbsp walnut oil

1 tsp Dijon mustard

salad greens, to serve

salt and pepper

1 Trim and discard the coarse, woody ends of the asparagus spears. Make sure all the stems are about the same length, then tie them together loosely with clean kitchen string. If you have an asparagus steamer, you don't need to tie the stems together—just place them in the basket.

2 Bring a tall pan of lightly salted water to a boil. Add the asparagus, making sure that the tips are protruding above the water, then reduce the heat and let simmer for 10–15 minutes, or until tender. Test by piercing a stem just above the water level with the point of a sharp knife. Drain, then refresh under cold running water and drain again.

3 Cut the asparagus spears into 1-inch/2.5-cm pieces, keeping the tips intact. Cut the artichoke hearts into small wedges and combine with the asparagus in a bowl.

4 Whisk the orange juice, orange rind, walnut oil, and mustard together in a bowl and season to taste with salt and pepper. If serving immediately, pour the

dressing over the artichoke hearts and asparagus and toss lightly.

5 Arrange the salad greens in individual serving dishes and top with the artichoke and asparagus mixture. Serve immediately. Alternatively, store the salad, covered, in the refrigerator and add the dressing just before serving.

Melon, Chorizo & Artichoke Salad

SERVES EIGHT

12 small globe artichokes
juice of ½ lemon
2 tbsp Spanish olive oil
1 small orange-fleshed melon,
   such as cantaloupe
7 oz/200 g chorizo sausage,
   outer casing removed
fresh tarragon or flatleaf
   parsley sprigs, to garnish

DRESSING

3 tbsp Spanish extra-virgin
   olive oil
1 tbsp red wine vinegar
1 tsp prepared mustard
1 tbsp chopped fresh
   tarragon
salt and pepper

1 To prepare the artichokes, cut off the stems. With your hands, break off the toughest outer leaves at the base until the tender inside leaves are visible. Using a pair of scissors, cut the spiky tips off the leaves. Using a sharp knife, pare the dark green skin from the base and down the stem. As you prepare them, brush the cut surfaces of the artichokes with lemon juice to prevent discoloration. Alternatively, you could fill a bowl with cold water to which you have added a little lemon juice, and immerse the artichokes in the acidulated water to stop discoloration. Carefully remove the choke (the mass of silky hairs) by pulling it out with your fingers or by scooping it out with a spoon. It is very important to remove all the choke, as the little barbs, if eaten, can irritate the throat. However, if you are using very young artichokes, you do not need to worry about removing the choke and you can include the stem too, well scraped, as it will be quite tender. Cut the artichokes into fourths and brush them again with lemon juice.

2 Heat the olive oil in a large, heavy-bottom skillet. Add the prepared artichokes and cook, stirring frequently, for 5 minutes, or until the artichoke leaves are golden brown. Remove from the skillet, then transfer to a large serving bowl and let cool.

3 To prepare the melon, cut in half and scoop out the seeds with a spoon. Cut the flesh into bite-size cubes. Add to the cooled artichokes. Cut the chorizo into bite-size chunks and add to the melon and artichokes.

4 To make the dressing, place all the ingredients in a small bowl and whisk together. Just before serving, pour the dressing over the prepared salad ingredients and toss together. Serve the salad garnished with tarragon or parsley sprigs.

VARIATION: You could use serrano ham, cut in one thick piece rather than sliced, instead of the chorizo.

Sautéed Garlic Mushrooms

SERVES SIX

1 lb/450 g white mushrooms

5 tbsp Spanish olive oil

2 garlic cloves, finely
   chopped

lemon juice

4 tbsp chopped fresh parsley

salt and pepper

lemon wedges, to garnish

crusty bread, to serve

VARIATION: Exotic mushrooms such as boletus or chanterelles can be used in place of cultivated mushrooms Zucchini may also be prepared in the same way with a finely chopped small onion cooked in the oil until lightly browned before adding the garlic.

1 Wipe or brush clean the mushrooms, then trim off the stems close to the caps. Cut any large mushrooms in half or into fourths. Heat the olive oil in a large, heavy-bottom skillet. Add the garlic and cook for 30 seconds– 1 minute, or until lightly browned. Add the mushrooms and sauté over high heat, stirring frequently, until the mushrooms have absorbed all the oil in the skillet.

2 Reduce the heat to low. When the juices have come out of the mushrooms, increase the heat again and sauté for 4–5 minutes, stirring frequently, until the juices have almost evaporated. Add a squeeze of lemon juice and season to taste with salt and pepper. Stir in the parsley and cook for an additional 1 minute.

3 Transfer the sautéed mushrooms to a warmed serving dish, then garnish with lemon wedges and serve piping hot or warm. Accompany with crusty bread for mopping up the juices.

Chili Mushrooms

SERVES SIX-EIGHT

½ stick butter

5 tbsp olive oil

2 lb 4 oz/1 kg white
   mushrooms

4 fat garlic cloves,
   finely chopped

1 fresh red chili, deseeded
   and finely chopped

1 tbsp lemon juice

salt and pepper

fresh parsley sprigs,
   to garnish

1 Heat the butter with the olive oil in a large, heavy-bottom skillet. When the butter has melted, add the mushrooms, garlic, and chili and cook over medium–low heat, stirring frequently, for 5 minutes.

2 Stir in the lemon juice and season to taste with salt and pepper.

3 Transfer to warmed serving dishes and serve immediately, garnished with parsley sprigs.

Stuffed Mushrooms

SERVES SIX

1½ sticks butter

4 garlic cloves, finely chopped

6 large open mushrooms, stems removed

1 cup fresh white bread crumbs

1 tbsp chopped fresh thyme

1 egg, lightly beaten

salt and pepper

1 Preheat the oven to 350°F/180°C. Cream the butter in a bowl until softened, then beat in the garlic. Divide two-thirds of the garlic butter between the mushroom caps and arrange them, cup-side up, on a baking sheet.

2 Melt the remaining garlic butter in a heavy-bottom or nonstick skillet. Add the bread crumbs and cook over low heat, stirring frequently, until golden. Remove from the heat and tip into a bowl. Stir in the thyme and season to taste with salt and pepper. Stir in the beaten egg until thoroughly combined.

3 Divide the bread-crumb mixture between the mushroom caps and bake in the preheated oven for 15 minutes, or until the stuffing is golden brown and the mushrooms are tender. Serve hot or warm.

COOK'S TIP: For a more substantial tapas, serve these mushrooms on toast. Stamp out circles of bread with a cookie cutter, then toast on both sides. Spread with butter or more garlic butter, then top each round with a stuffed mushroom.

Stuffed Bell Peppers

MAKES SIX

6 tbsp olive oil, plus a little extra for rubbing on bell peppers

2 onions, finely chopped

2 garlic cloves, crushed

²⁄₃ cup Spanish short-grain rice

¹⁄₃ cup raisins

¹⁄₃ cup pine nuts

generous ¹⁄₃ cup fresh parsley, finely chopped

1 tbsp tomato paste dissolved in 3 cups hot water

salt and pepper

4-6 red, green, or yellow bell peppers (or a mix of colors), or 6 of the long, Mediterranean variety

1 Preheat the oven to 400°F/200°C. Heat the oil in a shallow, heavy-bottom flameproof casserole. Add the onions and cook for 3 minutes. Add the garlic and cook for an additional 2 minutes, or until the onion is soft but not brown.

2 Stir in the rice, raisins, and pine nuts until all are coated in the oil, then add half the parsley and salt and pepper to taste. Stir in the tomato paste and bring to a boil. Reduce the heat and let simmer, uncovered, shaking the casserole frequently, for 20 minutes, or until the rice is tender, the liquid is absorbed and small holes appear on the surface. Watch carefully because the raisins can catch and burn. Stir in the remaining parsley, then let cool slightly.

3 While the rice is simmering, cut the top off each bell pepper and reserve. Remove the core and seeds from each bell pepper (see Cook's Tip).

4 Divide the stuffing equally between the bell peppers. Use wooden toothpicks to secure the tops back in place. Lightly rub each bell pepper with olive oil and arrange in a single layer in a baking dish. Bake in the preheated oven for 30 minutes, or until the bell peppers are tender. Serve hot or let cool to room temperature.

COOK'S TIP: If you are using the pointed, Mediterranean variety of pepper, a melon baller, teaspoon or small paring knife makes it easier to remove all the seeds.

Red Bell Peppers with Vinegar & Capers

SERVES SIX

1 tbsp capers

4 tbsp olive oil

2 lb 4 oz/1 kg red bell peppers, halved, deseeded and cut into strips

4 garlic cloves, finely chopped

2 tbsp sherry vinegar

salt and pepper

1 If using salted capers, brush off most of the salt with your fingers. If using pickled capers in vinegar, drain well and rinse thoroughly.

2 Heat the oil in a heavy-bottom skillet. Add the bell pepper strips and cook over medium heat, stirring frequently, for 10 minutes, or until softened and charred around the edges. Add the capers and garlic and cook for an additional 2–3 minutes.

3 Stir in the vinegar and season to taste with salt and pepper—season sparingly with salt if using salted capers. Cook for 1–2 minutes, then remove from the heat. Serve immediately or let cool. Cover and chill before serving.

COOK'S TIP: Capers preserved in salt are best for this dish; those preserved in vinegar are less suitable. If you can find them, try capers preserved in olive oil and use some of the oil from the jar for cooking.

Roasted Bell Peppers with Fiery Cheese

SERVES SIX

1 red bell pepper, halved and deseeded

1 orange bell pepper, halved and deseeded

1 yellow bell pepper, halved and deseeded

4 oz/115 g Afuega'l Pitu cheese or other hot spiced cheese, diced

1 tbsp clear honey

1 tbsp sherry vinegar

salt and pepper

1 Preheat the broiler to high. Place the bell peppers, skin-side up, in a single layer on a baking sheet. Cook under the hot broiler for 8–10 minutes, or until the skins have blistered and blackened. Using tongs, transfer to a plastic bag. Tie the top and let cool.

2 When the bell peppers are cool enough to handle, peel off the skin with your fingers or a knife and discard it. Place on a serving plate and sprinkle over the cheese.

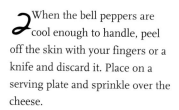

3 Whisk the honey and vinegar together in a bowl and season to taste with salt and pepper. Pour the dressing over the bell peppers, then cover and let chill until required.

COOK'S TIP: Afuega'l Pitu means "fire in the belly" and this is an apt description for the chili-flavored cheese from Asturias. If it is not available, you could use Hungarian Liptauer. Liptauer is spiced with paprika rather than chilies, but is still astonishingly spicy.

Pickled Stuffed Sweet Peppers

SERVES SIX

7 oz/200 g Cuajada cheese,
  Queso del Tietar or other
  goat's milk cheese
14 oz/400 g pickled sweet
  peppers or pimientos del
  piquillo, drained
1 tbsp finely chopped fresh
  dill
salt and pepper

COOK'S TIP: Pimientos del piquillo are available from delicatessens and some large supermarkets, but you can use any type of pickled pepper for this tapas. You can also make a spicier version with pickled chilies.

1 Cut the cheese into pieces about 1 cm/¹/2 inch long. Slit the sides of the sweet peppers and deseed, if you like. Stuff the peppers with the cheese.

2 Arrange the stuffed peppers on serving plates. Sprinkle with the dill and season to taste with salt and pepper. Cover and chill until required.

White Bean Vinaigrette

SERVES FOUR-SIX

14 oz/400 g canned wax
   beans
3 celery stalks, chopped
1 gherkin, finely chopped
⅔ cup olive oil
4 tbsp white wine vinegar
1 garlic clove, finely chopped
2 tsp Dijon mustard
1 tbsp chopped fresh parsley
pinch of sugar
salt and pepper
snipped fresh chives,
   to garnish

VARIATION: You can also
make this dish with other
types of white beans, such as
navy or cannellini.

1 Drain the beans and rinse well under cold running water, then drain again. Place the beans, celery, and gherkin in a bowl.

2 Whisk the olive oil, vinegar, garlic, mustard, parsley, and sugar together in a bowl and season to taste with salt and pepper.

3 Pour the vinaigrette over the bean mixture and toss well. Transfer to a serving dish and sprinkle with the chives, then serve at room temperature or cover and let chill before serving.

Empanadillas

SERVES SIX–EIGHT

2 tbsp olive oil, plus extra
   for brushing
1 lb 2 oz/500 g fresh spinach
   leaves
2 garlic cloves, finely
   chopped
8 canned anchovy fillets in
   oil, drained and chopped
2 tbsp raisins, soaked in hot
   water for 10 minutes
scant 1/3 cup pine nuts
1 lb/450 g puff pastry,
   thawed if frozen
all-purpose flour, for dusting
1 egg, lightly beaten
salt and pepper

1 Preheat the oven to 350°F/180°C. Lightly brush 1–2 baking sheets with olive oil.

2 Trim and discard any tough stems from the spinach and finely chop the leaves.

3 Heat the olive oil in a large pan. Add the chopped spinach, then cover and cook over low heat, gently shaking the pan occasionally, for 3 minutes. Stir in the garlic and anchovies and cook, uncovered, for an additional 1 minute. Remove the pan from the heat.

4 Drain the raisins and chop, then stir them into the spinach mixture with the pine nuts and salt and pepper to taste. Let cool.

5 Roll out the pastry on a lightly floured counter to a circle about 1/8 inch/3 mm thick. Stamp out circles using a 3-inch/7.5-cm biscuit cutter. Re-roll the trimmings and stamp out more circles.

6 Place 1–2 heaped teaspoonfuls of the spinach filling onto each pastry round. Brush the edges with water and fold over to make half moons. Press together well to seal. Place the empanadillas on the baking sheets and brush with beaten egg to glaze, then bake in the preheated oven for 15 minutes, or until golden brown. Serve warm.

COOK'S TIP: These little pastries originated in Galicia but are now made all over Spain and are extremely popular in South America, too.

Bandilleras

SERVES EIGHT-TEN

1 tbsp white wine vinegar
4 garlic cloves, finely chopped
1 fresh red chili, deseeded
  and finely chopped
1 tbsp sweet paprika
4 tbsp olive oil
3 skinless, boneless chicken
  breasts, cut into 1-inch/
  2.5-cm cubes
1 avocado
3 tbsp lemon juice
4 oz/115 g San Simon or other
  smoked cheese, diced
8-10 black olives, pitted
8-10 cherry tomatoes
3 oz/85 g Manchego or
  Cheddar cheese, cubed
8-10 pimiento-stuffed green
  olives
½ cantaloupe melon, deseeded
5-6 slices serrano ham

PICADA

4 garlic cloves, finely
  chopped
6 tbsp chopped fresh parsley
6 tbsp pickled cucumber,
  finely chopped
⅔ cup olive oil

1 Mix the vinegar, garlic, chili, paprika, and olive oil together in a bowl. Add the chicken and stir well to coat, then cover and let marinate in the refrigerator for at least 2 hours or preferably overnight.

2 Heat a large, heavy-bottom skillet. Tip the chicken mixture into the pan and cook over low heat, stirring frequently, for 10–15 minutes, or until cooked through. Remove from the heat and let cool to room temperature, then spear the chicken pieces with wooden toothpicks.

4 Scoop out 20 balls from the melon with a melon baller or teaspoon. Cut the ham into 20 strips and wrap around the melon balls. Thread the melon balls in pairs onto wooden toothpicks.

3 Peel and stone the avocado and cut into bite-size cubes. Toss in the lemon juice, then thread onto wooden toothpicks with the smoked cheese. Thread the black olives, tomatoes, Manchego cheese, and stuffed olives onto wooden toothpicks.

5 To make the Picada, mix all the ingredients together in a bowl until thoroughly combined into a fairly thick paste. Arrange all the filled toothpicks—bandilleras—on a large serving platter and serve with bowls of Picada.

Olives & Nuts

Spanish cooking is famous for its love of almonds and olives, so over the next few pages you will find a selection of dishes that are dedicated to these two essential ingredients.

If you're in the habit of inviting friends round for impromptu gatherings, having a jar or two of Marinated Olives (see page 84) in the pantry is a great way of having something tastier than store-bought chips and dips. The recipe for Salted Almonds (see page 89) is another famous nibble to serve with drinks, but it can be made equally well with other nuts—try walnut halves, pistachios, peanuts, or cashews for a change.

Marinated Olives

FILLS A 2-CUP
PRESERVING JAR

scant 1¼ cups green
   pimiento-stuffed Spanish
   olives in brine, rinsed
1 cup black Spanish olives
   in brine, rinsed
2 oz/55 g broiled and peeled
   bell pepper (see page 74),
   thinly sliced
2 thin lemon slices
2 fresh thyme sprigs
1 bay leaf
1 dried red chili
½ tsp fennel seeds
½ tsp coriander seeds,
   lightly cracked
extra-virgin olive oil

1 Place the olives, bell pepper strips, lemon slices, thyme, bay leaf, chili, and fennel and coriander seeds in a 2-cup preserving jar, making sure the ingredients are well mixed. Pour over enough olive oil to cover.

2 Seal the jar and let stand at room temperature for at least 2 weeks before using.

COOK'S TIP: Do not add sliced garlic to an oil marinade such as this, because of the possibility of botulism infection. For a garlic flavor, use a commercially prepared garlic-flavored olive oil. If you store the marinade in the refrigerator, the oil will become cloudy, but it clears again as it returns to room temperature.

Olives with Orange & Lemon

SERVES FOUR-SIX

2 tsp fennel seeds
2 tsp cumin seeds
1¼ cups green olives
1¼ cups black olives
2 tsp grated orange rind
2 tsp grated lemon rind
3 shallots, finely chopped
pinch of ground cinnamon
4 tbsp white wine vinegar
5 tbsp olive oil
2 tbsp orange juice
1 tbsp chopped fresh mint
1 tbsp chopped fresh parsley

COOK'S TIP: Look for Spanish varieties of olive—the aromatic arbequines, the large, green gordas del rey, the succulent manzanilla, or perlas from Aragon

1 Dry-fry the fennel seeds and cumin seeds in a small, heavy-bottom skillet, shaking the skillet frequently, until they begin to pop and give off their aroma. Remove the skillet from the heat and let cool.

2 Place the olives, orange and lemon rind, shallots, cinnamon, and toasted seeds in a bowl.

3 Whisk the vinegar, olive oil, orange juice, mint, and parsley together in a bowl and pour over the olives. Toss well, then cover and let chill for 1–2 days before serving.

Olives Wrapped with Anchovies

MAKES TWELVE

12 anchovy fillets in oil, drained

24 pimiento-stuffed green olives in oil, drained

VARIATION: Instead of using pimiento-stuffed olives, stuff pitted green or black olives with a blanched almond sliver. Proceed with the recipe as above.

1 Using a sharp knife, halve each anchovy fillet lengthwise.

2 Wrap a half fillet around the middle of each olive, over-lapping the ends, and secure with a wooden toothpick. Repeat with another olive and anchovy fillet half and slide onto the toothpick. Continue until all the ingredients are used. Serve immediately or cover until required.

Spicy Cracked Marinated Olives

SERVES EIGHT

1 lb/450 g canned or bottled unpitted large green olives, drained
4 garlic cloves, peeled
2 tsp coriander seeds
1 small lemon
4 fresh thyme sprigs
4 feathery stalks of fennel
2 small fresh red chilies (optional)
Spanish extra-virgin olive oil
pepper

1 To let the flavors of the marinade penetrate the olives, place on a cutting board and, using a rolling pin, bash them lightly so that they crack slightly. Alternatively, use a sharp knife to cut a lengthwise slit in each olive as far as the stone. Using the flat side of a broad knife, lightly crush each garlic clove. Using a pestle and mortar, crack the coriander seeds. Cut the lemon, with its rind, into small chunks.

2 Place the olives, garlic, coriander seeds, lemon chunks, thyme sprigs, fennel, and chilies, if using, in a large bowl and toss together. Season to taste with pepper, but you should not need to add salt as canned or bottled olives are usually salty enough. Pack the ingredients tightly into a glass jar with a lid. Pour in enough olive oil to cover the olives, then seal the jar tightly.

3 Let the olives stand at room temperature for 24 hours, then marinate in the refrigerator for at least 1 week but preferably 2 weeks before serving. From time to time, gently give the jar a shake to re-mix the ingredients. Return the olives to room temperature and remove from the oil to serve. Provide wooden toothpicks for spearing the olives.

Paprika-Spiced Almonds

MAKES 1 LB 2 OZ/500 G;
SERVES FOUR-SIX

1½ tbsp coarse sea salt
½ tsp smoked sweet Spanish
   paprika, or hot paprika,
   to taste
1 lb 2 oz/500 g blanched
   almonds
extra-virgin olive oil

1 Preheat the oven to 400°F/200°C. Place the sea salt and paprika in a mortar and grind with the pestle to a fine powder. Alternatively, use a mini spice blender (the amount is too small to process in a full-size processor).

2 Place the almonds on a baking sheet and toast in the preheated oven for 8–10 minutes, stirring occasionally, until golden and giving off a toasted aroma. Watch after 7 minutes because they burn quickly. Pour into a heatproof bowl.

3 Drizzle over 1 tablespoon of olive oil and stir to ensure all the nuts are lightly and evenly coated. Add extra oil, if necessary. Sprinkle with the salt and paprika mixture and stir again. Transfer to a small bowl and serve at room temperature.

Salted Almonds

SERVES SIX–EIGHT

8 oz/225 g whole almonds,
    in their skins or blanched
    (see method)
4 tbsp Spanish olive oil
coarse sea salt
1 tsp paprika or ground cumin
    (optional)

1 Preheat the oven to 350°F/180°C. Fresh almonds in their skins are superior in taste, but blanched almonds are much more convenient. If the almonds are not blanched, place them in a large bowl, cover with boiling water for 3–4 minutes, then plunge them into cold water for 1 minute. Drain them well in a strainer, then slide off the skins between your fingers. Dry the almonds well on paper towels.

2 Place the olive oil in a roasting pan and swirl it around so that it covers the base. Add the almonds and toss them in the pan so that they are evenly coated in the oil, then spread them out in a single layer.

3 Roast the almonds in the preheated oven for 20 minutes, or until they are light golden brown, tossing several times during the cooking. Drain the almonds on paper towels, then transfer them to a bowl.

4 While the almonds are still warm, sprinkle with plenty of sea salt and paprika, if using, and toss together to coat. Serve the almonds warm or cold. The almonds are at their best when served freshly cooked, so, if possible, cook them on the day that you plan to eat them. However, they can be stored in an airtight container for up to 3 days.

Eggs & Cheese

EGG-BASED DISHES FEATURE IN ALL TAPAS MENUS, AND YOU WILL FIND RECIPES FOR SUCH FAVORITES AS DEVILLED EGGS (SEE PAGE 96) AND SPANISH TORTILLA (SEE PAGE 100), FULL OF FLAVOR BUT USING VERY COMMON INGREDIENTS. OTHER TORTILLA RECIPES USE SPINACH OR CHORIZO FOR VARIETY, WHILE THE OVEN-BAKED TORTILLA (SEE PAGE 98), SERVED ON TOOTHPICKS IN THE BARS OF MADRID, MAKES A GREAT LIGHTER TAPAS DISH.

THERE IS A WIDE RANGE OF CHEESES, AND CHEESE DISHES, IN SPAIN, BUT IT CAN BE DIFFICULT TO BUY SOME OF THE MORE EXOTIC TYPES IN OTHER COUNTRIES. FOR THIS REASON, ALTERNATIVES ARE SUGGESTED WHERE THE LOCAL CHEESE IS LIKELY TO BE UNAVAILABLE.

Basque Scrambled Eggs

SERVES FOUR-SIX

3-4 tbsp olive oil

1 large onion, finely chopped

1 large red bell pepper, seeded and chopped

1 large green bell pepper, seeded and chopped

2 large tomatoes, peeled, seeded, (see page 167) and chopped

2 oz/55 g chorizo sausage, sliced thinly, outer casing removed, if preferred

generous ¼ stick butter

10 large eggs, lightly beaten

salt and pepper

4-6 thick slices country-style bread, toasted, to serve

1 Heat 2 tablespoons of olive oil in a large, heavy-bottom skillet over medium heat. Add the onion and bell peppers and cook for 5 minutes, or until the vegetables are softened but not browned. Add the tomatoes and heat through. Transfer to a heatproof plate and keep warm in a preheated low oven.

2 Add another tablespoon of oil to the skillet. Add the chorizo and cook for 30 seconds, just to warm through and flavor the oil. Add the sausage to the reserved vegetables.

3 Add a little extra olive oil, if necessary, to bring it back to 2 tablespoons. Add the butter and let melt. Season the eggs with salt and pepper, then add to the pan and scramble until cooked to the desired degree of firmness. Return the vegetables to the pan and stir through. Serve immediately with hot toast.

Basque Eggs with Bell Peppers

SERVES SIX

2 red bell peppers, halved and seeded

6 hard-cooked eggs, cooled, shelled, and sliced

2 tbsp white wine vinegar

5 tbsp olive oil

1 shallot, finely chopped

2 tsp chopped fresh dill

pinch of sugar

salt and pepper

1 Bring a pan of water to a boil. Add the bell peppers and blanch for 5 minutes. Drain, then refresh under cold running water and drain well again. Pat dry with paper towels and cut into thin strips.

2 Arrange the slices of egg on plates and sprinkle over the bell pepper strips. Alternatively, make a lattice pattern with the bell pepper strips.

3 Whisk the vinegar, olive oil, shallot, dill, and sugar together in a bowl and season to taste with salt and pepper. Spoon the dressing over the eggs and serve immediately.

Flamenco Eggs

SERVES FOUR

4 tbsp olive oil

1 onion, thinly sliced

2 garlic cloves, finely chopped

2 small red bell peppers,
    seeded and chopped

4 tomatoes, peeled, seeded
    (see page 167), and chopped

1 tbsp chopped fresh parsley

7 oz/200 g canned corn
    kernels, drained

4 eggs

salt and cayenne pepper

1 Preheat the oven to 350°F/180°C. Heat the olive oil in a large, heavy-bottom skillet. Add the onion and garlic and cook over low heat, stirring occasionally, for 5 minutes, or until softened. Add the red bell peppers and cook, stirring occasionally, for an additional 10 minutes. Stir in the tomatoes and parsley, season to taste with salt and cayenne and cook for an additional 5 minutes. Stir in the corn kernels and remove the skillet from the heat.

2 Divide the mixture between 4 individual ovenproof dishes. Make a hollow in the surface of each using the back of a spoon. Break an egg into each depression.

3 Bake in the preheated oven for 15–25 minutes, or until the eggs have set. Serve hot.

COOK'S TIP: If you prefer, you can also cook the eggs in a single ovenproof dish and serve at the table. In this case, you may need to cook them for slightly longer.

Devilled Eggs

MAKES SIXTEEN

8 large eggs
2 whole canned or bottled
   pimientos del piquillo
   (charbroiled sweet red
   peppers)
8 green olives
5 tbsp mayonnaise
8 drops Tabasco sauce
large pinch of cayenne
   pepper
salt and pepper
paprika, for dusting
fresh dill sprigs, to garnish

1 To cook the eggs, place them in a pan, then cover with cold water and slowly bring to a boil. Immediately reduce the heat to very low, then cover and simmer gently for 10 minutes. As soon as the eggs are cooked, drain and place under cold running water until they are cold. By doing this quickly, it will prevent a black ring forming around the egg yolk. Gently tap the eggs to crack the eggshells and let stand until cold. When cold, crack the shells and remove them.

2 Using a stainless steel knife, halve the eggs lengthwise, then carefully remove the yolks. Place the yolks in a nylon strainer set over a bowl and rub through, then mash them with a wooden spoon or fork. If necessary, rinse the egg whites under cold running water and dry carefully.

3 Place the pimientos on paper towels to dry well, then chop them finely, reserving a few strips. Finely chop the olives. If you are going to pipe the filling into the eggs, you need to chop both these ingredients very finely so that they will go through a $^{1}/_{2}$-inch/1-cm nozzle. Add the chopped pimientos and most of the chopped olives to the mashed egg yolks, reserving 16 larger pieces to garnish. Add the mayonnaise, mix together well, then add the Tabasco, cayenne, and salt and pepper to taste.

4 For a grand finale, place the egg yolk mixture into a pastry bag fitted with a $^{1}/_{2}$-inch/1-cm plain tip and pipe the mixture into the hollow egg whites. Alternatively, for a simpler finish, use a teaspoon to spoon the prepared filling into each egg half.

5 Arrange the eggs on a serving plate. Add a small strip of the reserved pimientos and a piece of olive to the top of each stuffed egg. Dust with a little paprika and garnish with dill sprigs, then serve.

Stuffed Eggs

SERVES SIX

6 hard-cooked eggs, cooled
  and shelled
4 1/4 oz/120 g canned sardines
  in olive oil, drained
4 tbsp lemon juice
  dash of Tabasco sauce
1-2 tbsp mayonnaise
1/3 cup all-purpose flour
1 1/2 cups fresh white bread
  crumbs
1 large egg, lightly beaten
vegetable oil, for deep-frying
salt and pepper
fresh parsley sprigs, to
  garnish

1 Cut the eggs in half lengthwise and, using a teaspoon, carefully scoop out the yolks into a fine strainer, reserving the egg white halves. Rub the yolks through the strainer into a bowl.

2 Mash the sardines with a fork, then mix with the egg yolks. Stir in the lemon juice and Tabasco, then add enough mayonnaise to make a paste. Season to taste with salt and pepper.

3 Spoon the filling into the egg white halves, mounding it up well. Spread out the flour and bread crumbs in separate shallow dishes. Dip each egg half first in the flour, then in the beaten egg and finally in the bread crumbs.

4 Heat the vegetable oil for deep-frying in a deep-fat fryer or large pan to 350–375°F/180–190°C, or until a cube of bread browns in 30 seconds. Deep-fry the egg halves, in batches if necessary, for 2 minutes, or until golden brown. Drain on paper towels and serve hot, garnished with parsley sprigs.

Oven-Baked Tortilla

MAKES FORTY-EIGHT PIECES

olive oil

1 large garlic clove, crushed

4 scallions, white and green
parts finely chopped

1 green bell pepper, seeded
and finely diced

1 red bell pepper, seeded
and finely diced

6 oz/175 g potato, boiled,
peeled, and diced

5 large eggs

scant ⅓ cup sour cream

6 oz/175 g freshly grated
Spanish Roncal cheese, or
Cheddar or Parmesan
cheese

3 tbsp snipped fresh chives

salt and pepper

green salad, to serve

1 Preheat the oven to 375°F/190°C. Line a 7 x 10-inch/18 x 25-cm baking sheet with foil and brush with the olive oil. Reserve.

2 Place a little olive oil, the garlic, scallions, and peppers in a skillet and cook over medium heat, stirring, for 10 minutes, or until the onions are softened but not browned. Let cool, then stir in the potato.

3 Beat the eggs, sour cream, cheese, and chives together in a large bowl. Stir the cooled vegetables into the bowl and season to taste with salt and pepper.

4 Pour the mixture into the baking sheet and smooth over the top. Bake in the preheated oven for 30–40 minutes, or until golden brown, puffed and set in the center. Remove from the oven and let cool and set. Run a spatula around the edge, then invert onto a cutting board, browned-side up, and peel off the foil. If the surface looks a little runny, place it under a medium broiler to dry out.

5 Let cool completely. Trim the edges if necessary, then cut into 48 squares. Serve on a platter with wooden toothpicks, or secure each square to a slice of bread, and accompany with a green salad.

Spanish Tortilla

MAKES EIGHT-TEN SLICES

½ cup olive oil
1 lb 5 oz/600 g potatoes,
   peeled and thinly sliced
1 large onion, thinly sliced
6 large eggs
salt and pepper
fresh flatleaf parsley, to
   garnish

1 Heat a nonstick 10-inch/25-cm skillet over high heat. Add the olive oil and heat. Reduce the heat, then add the potatoes and onion and cook for 15–20 minutes, or until the potatoes are tender.

2 Beat the eggs in a large bowl and season generously with salt and pepper. Drain the potatoes and onion through a strainer over a heatproof bowl to reserve the oil. Very gently stir the vegetables into the eggs, then let stand for 10 minutes.

3 Use a wooden spoon or spatula to remove any crusty bits stuck to the base of the skillet. Reheat the skillet over medium heat with 4 tablespoons of the reserved oil. Add the egg mixture and smooth the surface, pressing the potatoes and onions into an even layer.

4 Cook for 5 minutes, shaking the skillet occasionally, until the base is set. Use a spatula to loosen the side of the tortilla. Place a large plate over the top and carefully invert the skillet and plate together so the tortilla drops onto the plate.

5 Add 1 tablespoon of the remaining reserved oil to the skillet and swirl around. Carefully slide the tortilla back into the skillet, cooked-side up. Run the spatula around the tortilla, to tuck in the edge.

6 Continue cooking for 3 minutes, or until the eggs are set and the base is golden brown. Remove the skillet from the heat and slide the tortilla onto a plate. Let stand for at least 5 minutes before cutting. Garnish with parsley and serve.

Spinach & Mushroom Tortilla

SERVES FOUR

2 tbsp olive oil

3 shallots, finely chopped

12 oz/350 g mushrooms, sliced

10 oz/280 g fresh spinach leaves, coarse stems removed

2 oz/55 g toasted slivered almonds

5 eggs

2 tbsp chopped fresh parsley

2 tbsp cold water

3 oz/85 g mature Mahon (see Cook's Tip, page 106), Manchego, or Parmesan cheese, grated

salt and pepper

1 Heat the olive oil in a skillet that can safely be placed under the broiler. Add the shallots and cook over low heat, stirring occasionally, for 5 minutes, or until softened. Add the mushrooms and cook, stirring frequently, for an additional 4 minutes. Add the spinach, then increase the heat to medium and cook, stirring frequently, for 3–4 minutes, or until wilted. Reduce the heat, then season to taste with salt and pepper and stir in the slivered almonds.

2 Beat the eggs with the parsley, water, and salt and pepper to taste in a bowl. Pour the mixture into the skillet and cook for 5–8 minutes, or until the underside is set. Lift the edge of the tortilla occasionally to let the uncooked egg run underneath. Meanwhile, preheat the broiler to high.

3 Sprinkle the grated cheese over the tortilla and cook under the preheated hot broiler for 3 minutes, or until the top is set and the cheese has melted. Serve, lukewarm or cold, cut into thin wedges.

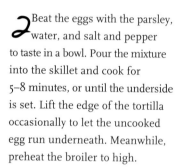

Chorizo & Cheese Tortilla

SERVES EIGHT

2 small potatoes
4 tbsp olive oil
1 small onion, chopped
1 red bell pepper, seeded
    and chopped
2 tomatoes, seeded and
    diced
5 oz/140 g chorizo sausage,
    finely chopped
8 large eggs
2 tbsp cold water
2 oz/55 g mature Mahon
    (see Cook's Tip, page 106),
    Manchego, or Parmesan
    cheese, grated
salt and pepper

1 Cook the potatoes in a small pan of lightly salted boiling water for 15–20 minutes, or until just tender. Drain and let stand until cool enough to handle, then dice.

2 Heat the olive oil in a large skillet that can safely be placed under the broiler. Add the onion, bell pepper, and tomatoes and cook over low heat, stirring occasionally, for 5 minutes. Add the diced potatoes and chorizo and cook for an additional 5 minutes. Meanwhile, preheat the broiler to high.

3 Beat the eggs with the water and salt and pepper to taste in a large bowl. Pour the mixture into the skillet and cook for 8–10 minutes, or until the underside is set. Lift the edge of the tortilla occasionally to let the uncooked egg run underneath. Sprinkle the grated cheese over the tortilla and place under the hot broiler for 3 minutes, or until the top is set and the cheese has melted. Serve, warm or cold, cut into thin wedges.

Baked Tomato Nests

SERVES FOUR

4 large ripe tomatoes

4 large eggs

4 tbsp heavy cream

4 tbsp grated mature
  Mahon, Manchego, or
  Parmesan cheese

salt and pepper

1 Preheat the oven to 350°F/180°C. Cut a slice off the tops of the tomatoes and, using a teaspoon, carefully scoop out the pulp and seeds without piercing the shells. Turn the tomato shells upside down on paper towels and let drain for 15 minutes. Season the insides of the shells with salt and pepper.

2 Place the tomatoes in an ovenproof dish just large enough to hold them in a single layer. Carefully break 1 egg into each tomato shell, then top with 1 tablespoon of cream and 1 tablespoon of grated cheese.

3 Bake in the preheated oven for 15–20 minutes, or until the eggs are just set. Serve hot.

COOK'S TIP: Mahon cheese, from Minorca in the Balearic Islands, is the Spanish equivalent of Parmesan—a hard cheese with a grainy texture.

Eggs & Cheese

SERVES SIX

6 hard-cooked eggs, cooled
  and shelled
3 tbsp grated Manchego or
  Cheddar cheese
1-2 tbsp mayonnaise
2 tbsp snipped fresh chives
1 fresh red chili, seeded and
  finely chopped
salt and pepper
lettuce leaves, to serve

VARIATION: For a special
occasion, use quails' eggs—you
will need about 18. Boil them
for 3-4 minutes, refresh
under cold running water
and shell immediately.

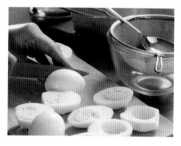

1 Cut the eggs in half lengthwise and, using a teaspoon, carefully scoop out the yolks into a fine strainer, reserving the egg white halves. Rub the yolks through the strainer into a bowl and add the grated cheese, mayonnaise, chives, chili, and salt and pepper to taste.

2 Spoon the filling into the egg white halves.

3 Arrange a bed of lettuce on individual serving plates and top with the eggs. Cover and let chill until ready to serve.

Figs with Blue Cheese

SERVES SIX
CARAMELIZED ALMONDS
½ cup superfine sugar
4 oz/115 g whole almonds
butter, for greasing
TO SERVE
12 ripe figs
12 oz/350 g Spanish blue
  cheese, such as Picós,
  crumbled
extra-virgin olive oil

VARIATION: Walnut halves can also be caramelized and used in this recipe.

1 First make the caramelized almonds. Place the sugar in a pan over medium heat and stir until the sugar melts and turns golden brown and bubbles. Do not stir once the mixture begins to bubble. Remove the pan from the heat, then add the almonds one at a time and quickly turn with a fork until coated. If the caramel hardens, return the pan to the heat. Transfer each almond to a lightly greased baking sheet once it is coated. Let stand until cool and firm.

2 To serve, slice the figs in half and arrange 4 halves on individual serving plates. Coarsely chop the almonds by hand. Place a mound of blue cheese on each plate and sprinkle with chopped almonds. Drizzle the figs very lightly with the olive oil.

Cheese & Olive Empanadillas

MAKES TWENTY-SIX

3 oz/85 g firm or soft
  cheese (see Cook's Tip)
1/2 cup pitted green olives
1/3 cup sun-dried tomatoes
  in oil, drained
1 3/4 oz/50 g canned anchovy
  fillets, drained
2 oz/55 g sun-dried tomato
  paste
1 lb 2 oz/500 g ready-made
  puff pastry, thawed if
  frozen
all-purpose flour, for dusting
beaten egg, to glaze
pepper
fresh flatleaf parsley sprigs,
  to garnish

1 Preheat the oven to 400°F/200°C. Cube the cheese into small dice measuring about 1/4 inch/5 mm. Chop the olives, sun-dried tomatoes, and anchovies into pieces about the same size as the cheese. Place all the chopped ingredients in a bowl, then season to taste with pepper and gently mix together. Stir in the sun-dried tomato paste.

2 Thinly roll out the puff pastry on a lightly floured counter. Using a plain, round 3 1/4-inch/8-cm cutter, cut into 18 circles. Gently pile the trimmings together and roll out again, then cut out an additional 8 circles. Using a teaspoon, place a little of the prepared filling equally in the center of each of the pastry circles.

3 Dampen the edges of the pastry with a little water, then bring up the sides to completely cover the filling and pinch the edges together with your fingers to seal them. With the point of a sharp knife, make a small slit in the top of each pastry. You can store the pastries in the refrigerator at this stage until you are ready to bake them.

4 Place the pastries onto dampened baking sheets and brush each with a little beaten egg to glaze. Bake in the preheated oven for 10–15 minutes, or until golden brown, crisp, and well risen. Serve the empanadillas piping hot, warm or cold, garnished with parsley sprigs.

COOK'S TIP: Since there are not many Spanish cheeses available outside Spain, you can make these pastries with Manchego, Cheddar, Gruyère, Gouda, mozzarella, or a firm goat cheese.

Cheese Puffs with Fiery Tomato Salsa

SERVES EIGHT

½ cup all-purpose flour
¼ cup Spanish olive oil
⅔ cup water
2 eggs, beaten
2 oz/55 g Manchego,
  Parmesan, Cheddar,
  Gouda, or Gruyère
  cheese, finely grated
½ tsp paprika
corn oil, for deep-frying
salt and pepper

FIERY TOMATO SALSA

2 tbsp Spanish olive oil
1 small onion, finely chopped
1 garlic clove, crushed
splash of dry white wine
14 oz/400 g canned chopped
  tomatoes
1 tbsp tomato paste
¼–½ tsp chili flakes
dash of Tabasco sauce
pinch of sugar
salt and pepper

1 To make the salsa, heat the olive oil in a pan. Add the onion and cook for 5 minutes, or until softened but not browned. Add the garlic and cook for an additional 30 seconds. Add the wine and let bubble, then add all the remaining salsa ingredients to the pan and simmer, uncovered, for 10–15 minutes, or until a thick sauce has formed. Spoon into a serving bowl and reserve until ready to serve.

2 Meanwhile, prepare the cheese puffs. Sift the flour onto a plate or sheet of waxed paper. Place the olive oil and water in a pan and slowly bring to a boil. As soon as the water boils, remove from the heat and quickly tip in the flour all at once. Using a wooden spoon, beat the mixture until it is smooth and leaves the sides of the pan.

3 Let the mixture cool for 1–2 minutes. Gradually add the eggs, beating hard after each addition and keeping the mixture stiff. Add the cheese and paprika, then season to taste with salt and pepper and mix well. Store in a refrigerator until you are ready to cook the cheese puffs.

4 Just before serving the cheese puffs, heat the sunflower oil in a deep-fat fryer to 350–375°F/180–190°C, or until a cube of bread browns in 30 seconds. Drop teaspoonfuls of the prepared mixture, in batches, into the hot oil and deep-fry for 2–3 minutes, turning once, or until golden brown and crispy. They should rise to the surface of the oil and puff up. Drain well on paper towels.

5 Serve the puffs piping hot, accompanied by the fiery salsa for dipping and wooden toothpicks to spear the puffs.

Burgos with Sherry Vinegar

SERVES FOUR
14 oz/400 g Burgos cheese
1-2 tbsp clear honey
3 tbsp sherry vinegar
TO SERVE
carrot sticks
chilled sherry

COOK'S TIP: Burgos, named after the Castilian city where it is produced, is a pure white, unpasteurized cheese made from cow's and/or sheep's milk. Cuajada, from northern Navarre, is similar, but if you can't find either, mascarpone, a widely available Italian cheese, may be substituted.

1 Place the cheese in a bowl and beat until smooth, then beat in 1 tablespoon of the honey and 1¹/2 tablespoons of the vinegar.

2 Taste and adjust the sweetness to your liking by adding more honey or more vinegar as required.

3 Divide between 4 small serving bowls, then cover and let chill until required. Serve with carrot sticks and chilled sherry.

Fried Manchego Cheese

SERVES SIX-EIGHT

7 oz/200 g Manchego cheese
3 tbsp all-purpose flour
1 egg
1 tsp water
1 ½ cups fresh white or
    brown bread crumbs
corn oil, for deep-frying
salt and pepper

1 Slice the cheese into triangular shapes about 2 cm/3/4 inch thick or alternatively into cubes measuring about the same size. Place the flour in a plastic bag and season to taste with salt and pepper. Break the egg into a shallow dish and beat together with the water. Spread the bread crumbs onto a large plate.

2 Toss the cheese pieces in the flour so that they are evenly coated, then dip the cheese in the egg mixture. Finally, dip the cheese in the bread crumbs so that the pieces are coated on all sides. Transfer to a large plate and store in the refrigerator until you are ready to serve them.

3 Just before serving, heat about 1 inch/2.5 cm of the corn oil in a large, heavy-bottom skillet or deep-fat fryer to 350–375°F/180–190°C, or until a cube of bread browns in 30 seconds. Add the cheese pieces, in batches of about 4 or 5 pieces so that the temperature of the oil

does not drop, and deep-fry for 1–2 minutes, turning once, until the cheese is just beginning to melt and they are golden brown on all sides. Do make sure that the oil is hot enough, otherwise the coating on the cheese will take too long to become crisp and the cheese inside may ooze out.

4 Using a slotted spoon, remove the fried cheese from the skillet or deep-fat fryer and drain well on paper towels. Serve the fried cheese pieces hot, accompanied by wooden toothpicks on which to spear them.

Bean & Cabrales Salad

SERVES FOUR

scant 1 cup small dried
  great Northern beans,
  soaked for
  4 hours or overnight
1 bay leaf
4 tbsp olive oil
2 tbsp sherry vinegar
2 tsp clear honey
1 tsp Dijon mustard
salt and pepper
2 tbsp toasted slivered
  almonds
7 oz/200 g Cabrales or
  other blue cheese,
  crumbled

1 Drain the beans and place in a large, heavy-bottom pan. Pour in enough water to cover, then add the bay leaf and bring to a boil. Boil for 1–1^{1}/2 hours, or until tender. Drain, then tip into a bowl and let cool slightly. Remove and discard the bay leaf.

2 Meanwhile, make the dressing. Whisk the olive oil, vinegar, honey, and mustard together in a bowl and season to taste with salt and pepper. Pour the dressing over the beans and toss lightly. Add the almonds and toss lightly again. Let cool to room temperature.

3 Spoon the beans into individual serving bowls and scatter over the cheese before serving.

Cheese & Shallots with Herb Dressing

SERVES SIX

1 tsp sesame seeds
¼ tsp cumin seeds
4 tomatoes, seeded and
  diced
5 tbsp olive oil
4 tbsp lemon juice
2 tsp chopped fresh thyme
1 tbsp chopped fresh mint
4 shallots, finely chopped
1 lb 2 oz/500 g Idiazabal or
  other sheep's milk cheese,
  diced
salt and pepper

1 Dry-fry the sesame and cumin seeds in a small, heavy-bottom skillet, shaking the skillet frequently, until they begin to pop and give off their aroma. Remove the skillet from the heat and let cool.

2 Place the tomatoes in a bowl. To make the dressing, whisk the olive oil and lemon juice together in a separate bowl. Season to taste with salt and pepper, then add the thyme, mint, and shallots and mix well.

3 Place the cheese in another bowl. Pour half the dressing over the tomatoes and toss lightly. Cover with plastic wrap and let chill for 1 hour. Pour the remaining dressing over the cheese, then cover and chill for 1 hour.

4 To serve, divide the cheese mixture between 6 serving plates and sprinkle with half the toasted seeds. Top with the tomato mixture and sprinkle with the remaining toasted seeds.

Manchego with Membrillo

SERVES SIX

12 oz/350 g Manchego
  cheese, sliced

MEMBRILLO

1 lb 2 oz/500 g quinces
4 cups water
preserving sugar (see
  method)

1 To make the membrillo, coarsely chop the unpeeled quinces and place in a large, heavy-bottom pan. Add the water and bring to a boil over high heat. Reduce the heat and simmer gently for 45 minutes, or until the fruit is very tender.

2 Pour the mixture into a jelly bag set over a bowl. Alternatively, loosely but securely tie a large cheesecloth square to the legs of an upturned stool, then place a bowl underneath and pour the mixture into the square. Let stand for at least 8 hours to enable the juice to drip through. Do not squeeze or the jelly will be cloudy.

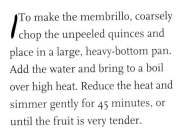

3 Measure the juice and pour it into a large, heavy-bottom pan. Add 1 lb 2 oz/500 g preserving sugar for each 2^1/2 cups of juice. Bring the mixture to a boil over medium heat, stirring until the sugar has dissolved. Increase the heat and boil rapidly until the temperature on a sugar thermometer measures 220°F/104°C. If you don't have a sugar thermometer, remove the pan from the heat and place a spoonful of the mixture on a chilled saucer to test. Let stand in a cool place for a few minutes. If a skin forms that can be wrinkled by pushing with your finger, the jelly is ready. Otherwise, return the pan to the heat for 1 minute, then test again.

4 Ladle the jelly into warmed, sterilized jars. Cover and seal. Label the jars when cold and store in a cool, dark place until required.

5 To serve, arrange slices of Manchego cheese on serving plates and add a generous 2 tablespoons of membrillo.

Fish & Seafood

FISH AND SEAFOOD HAVE ENJOYED A RICH TRADITION IN SPANISH CUISINE. THIS HAS BEEN HELPED BY THE FACT THAT THE COUNTRY IS BORDERED BY BOTH THE ATLANTIC AND THE MEDITERRANEAN AND ALSO INCLUDES A NUMBER OF ISLANDS.

THIS CHAPTER REFLECTS THE REGIONAL DIFFERENCES IN THE DISHES, WITH RECIPES FOR BROILED SARDINES (SEE PAGE 138), A POPULAR DISH ALL ALONG THE MEDITERRANEAN COAST, AND FRESH SALMON IN MOJO SAUCE (SEE PAGE 130) FROM THE CANARY ISLANDS. DRIED SALT COD, A BASQUE FAVORITE, IS USED IN SALT COD FRITTERS WITH SPINACH (SEE PAGE 122). THERE IS ALSO A VARIETY OF RECIPES FOR SHRIMP (SEE PAGES 162–74), WHICH ARE ENJOYED THROUGHOUT THE COUNTRY, AND, OF COURSE, THERE IS A RECIPE FOR MAKING CALAMARI (SEE PAGE 152).

Salt Cod Fritters with Spinach

MAKES ABOUT SIXTEEN

9 oz/250 g dried salt cod in
  1 piece

BATTER

1 cup all-purpose flour
1 tsp baking powder
1/4 tsp salt
1 large egg, lightly beaten
about 2/3 cup milk
2 lemon slices
2 fresh parsley sprigs
1 bay leaf
1/2 tbsp garlic-flavored olive oil
3 oz/85 g fresh baby spinach,
  rinsed
1/4 tsp smoked sweet, mild or
  hot Spanish paprika,
  to taste
olive oil
coarse sea salt (optional)
1 quantity Aioli (see page 12),
  garnished with fresh
  flatleaf parsley sprig,
  to serve

1 Place the dried salt cod in a large bowl. Cover with cold water and let soak for 48 hours, changing the water at least 3 times a day.

2 Meanwhile, make the batter. Sift the flour, baking powder, and salt into a large bowl and make a well. Mix the egg with scant 1/2 cup of the milk and pour into the well in the flour, stirring to make a smooth batter with a thick coating consistency. If it seems too thick, gradually stir in the remaining milk, then let stand for at least 1 hour.

3 After the salt cod has soaked, transfer it to a large skillet. Add the lemon slices, parsley sprigs, bay leaf, and enough water to cover and bring to a boil. Reduce the heat and simmer for 30–45 minutes, or until the fish is tender and flakes easily.

4 Meanwhile, prepare the spinach. Heat the garlic-flavored olive oil in a small pan over medium heat. Add the spinach with just the water clinging to the leaves and cook for 3–4 minutes, or until wilted.

5 Drain the spinach in a strainer, using the back of a spoon to press out any excess moisture. Finely chop the spinach, then stir it into the batter with the paprika.

6 Remove the fish from the water and flake the flesh into pieces, removing all the skin and tiny bones. Stir the flesh into the batter.

7 Heat 2 inches/5 cm of olive oil in a heavy-bottom skillet to 350–375°F/180–190°C, or until a cube of bread browns in 30 seconds. Use a greased tablespoon or measuring spoon to drop spoonfuls of the batter into the oil, then cook for 8–10 minutes, or until golden brown. Work in batches to avoid crowding the skillet. Use a slotted spoon to transfer the fritters to paper towels to drain and sprinkle with sea salt, if using.

8 Serve hot or at room temperature with Aïoli for dipping.

Traditional Catalan Salt Cod Salad

SERVES FOUR-SIX

14 oz/400 g dried salt cod in
    1 piece
6 scallions, thinly sliced on
    the diagonal
6 tbsp extra-virgin olive oil
1 tbsp sherry vinegar
1 tbsp lemon juice
2 large red bell peppers,
    broiled, peeled (see page 74),
    seeded, and very finely
    diced
12 large black olives, pitted
    and sliced
2 large, juicy tomatoes,
    thinly sliced
pepper
2 tbsp very finely chopped
    fresh parsley, to garnish

1 Place the dried salt cod in a large bowl, then cover with cold water and let soak for 48 hours, changing the water 3 times a day.

2 Pat the salt cod very dry with paper towels and remove the skin and bones, then use your fingers to tear into fine shreds. Place in a large, nonmetallic bowl with the scallions, olive oil, vinegar, and lemon juice and toss together. Season with pepper, then cover and let marinate in the refrigerator for 3 hours.

3 Stir in the bell peppers and olives. Taste and adjust the seasoning, if necessary, remembering that the cod and olives might be salty. Arrange the tomato slices on a large serving platter or individual serving plates and spoon the salad on top. Sprinkle with chopped parsley and serve.

Fried Salt Cod

SERVES SIX

12 oz/350 g dried salt cod
2½ cups milk
vegetable oil, for deep-frying
all-purpose flour, for dusting
sea salt
lemon wedges, to garnish
Romesco Sauce (see page 141),
    to serve (optional)

1 Soak the dried salt cod in cold water for 48 hours, changing the water 3 times a day.

2 Bring the milk to a boil in a pan, then remove from the heat and let cool completely.

3 Drain the fish and pat dry with paper towels, then cut into short strips, removing and discarding any skin and bones. Place the fish pieces in a bowl and pour over the cooled milk. Cover and let soak in a cool place or the refrigerator for 1 hour.

4 Drain the fish, discarding the milk, and pat dry with paper towels. Heat the vegetable oil in a deep-fat fryer or large pan to 350–375°F/180–190°C, or until a cube of bread browns in 30 seconds. Meanwhile, dust the fish pieces with flour, shaking off the excess.

5 Deep-fry the fish pieces, in batches if necessary, for 2–4 minutes, or until golden brown. Drain on paper towels and sprinkle generously with sea salt. When all the fish is cooked, transfer to warmed serving plates, then garnish with lemon wedges and serve with bowls of Romesco Sauce, if you like.

Salt Cod & Avocado

SERVES SIX

12 oz/350 g dried salt cod
2 tbsp olive oil
1 onion, finely chopped
1 garlic clove, finely chopped
3 avocados
1 tbsp lemon juice
pinch of chili powder
1 tbsp dry sherry
4 tbsp heavy cream
salt and pepper

1 Soak the dried salt cod in cold water for 48 hours, changing the water 3 times a day. Drain well and pat dry on paper towels, then chop.

2 Preheat the oven to 350°F/180°C. Heat the olive oil in a large, heavy-bottom skillet. Add the onion and garlic and cook over low heat, stirring occasionally, for 5 minutes, or until softened. Add the fish and cook over medium heat, stirring frequently, for 6–8 minutes, or until the fish flakes easily. Remove the skillet from the heat and let cool slightly.

3 Meanwhile, halve the avocados lengthwise and remove and discard the pits. Using a teaspoon, carefully scoop out the flesh without piercing the shells. Reserve the shells and mash the flesh with the lemon juice in a bowl.

4 Remove and discard any skin and bones from the fish, then add the fish mixture to the avocado, together with the chili powder, sherry, and cream. Beat well with a fork and season to taste with salt and pepper.

5 Spoon the mixture into the avocado shells and place them on a baking sheet. Bake in the preheated oven for 10–15 minutes, then transfer to warmed serving plates and serve.

Cod & Caper Croquettes

MAKES TWELVE

12 oz/350 g white fish fillets,
   such as cod, haddock or
   monkfish
1¼ cups milk
4 tbsp olive oil or ½ stick
   butter
⅓ cup all-purpose flour
4 tbsp capers, coarsely
   chopped
1 tsp paprika
1 garlic clove, crushed
1 tsp lemon juice
3 tbsp chopped fresh
   flatleaf parsley,
   plus extra sprigs
   to garnish
1 egg, beaten
1 cup fresh white bread
   crumbs
1 tbsp sesame seeds
corn oil, for deep-frying
salt and pepper
lemon wedges, to garnish
mayonnaise, to serve

1 Place the fish in a large skillet. Pour in the milk and season to taste. Bring to a boil, then reduce the heat and simmer, covered, for 8–10 minutes, or until the fish flakes easily. Using a spatula, remove the fish from the skillet. Pour the milk into a pitcher and reserve. Flake the fish, discarding the skin and bones.

2 Heat the olive oil in a large pan. Stir in the flour to form a paste and cook gently, stirring, for 1 minute. Remove from the heat and gradually stir in the reserved milk until smooth. Return to the heat and slowly bring to a boil, stirring, until the mixture thickens.

3 Remove from the heat, then add the fish and beat until smooth. Add the capers, paprika, garlic, lemon juice and parsley and mix. Season to taste. Spread the fish mixture in a dish and let stand until cool, then cover and chill for 2–3 hours or overnight.

4 When the fish mixture has chilled, pour the beaten egg onto a plate. Place the bread crumbs and sesame seeds on a separate plate, then mix together and spread out. Divide the fish mixture into 12 portions. Then, with lightly floured hands, form each portion into a sausage shape, 3 inches/7.5 cm in length. Dip the croquettes, one at a time, in the beaten egg and roll in the bread-crumb mixture. Place on a plate and chill for 1 hour.

5 Heat the corn oil in a deep-fat fryer to 350–375°F/180–190°C, or until a cube of bread browns in 30 seconds. Add the croquettes, in batches, and deep-fry for 3 minutes, or until golden and crispy. Remove with a slotted spoon and drain on paper towels. Serve hot, garnished with lemon wedges and parsley sprigs, with mayonnaise for dipping.

Fresh Salmon in Mojo Sauce

SERVES EIGHT

4 fresh salmon fillets,
  weighing about
  1 lb 10 oz/750 g in total
3 tbsp Spanish olive oil
salt and pepper
1 fresh flatleaf parsley sprig,
  to garnish

MOJO SAUCE

2 garlic cloves, peeled
2 tsp paprika
1 tsp ground cumin
5 tbsp Spanish extra-virgin
  olive oil
2 tbsp white wine vinegar
salt

1 To prepare the sauce, place the garlic, paprika, and cumin in a food processor fitted with a metal blade and, using a pulsing action, process for 1 minute to mix well. With the motor still running, add 1 tablespoon of the olive oil, drop by drop, through the feeder tube. When it has been added, scrape down the sides of the bowl with a spatula, then very slowly continue to pour in the oil in a thin, steady stream, until all the oil has been added and the sauce has slightly thickened. Add the vinegar and process for an additional 1 minute. Season the sauce to taste with salt.

2 To prepare the salmon, remove the skin and cut each fillet in half widthwise, then cut lengthwise into 3/4-inch/2-cm thick slices, discarding any bones. Season the pieces of fish to taste with salt and pepper.

3 Heat the olive oil in a large, heavy-bottom skillet. When hot, add the pieces of fish and cook for 10 minutes, depending on its thickness, turning occasionally until cooked and browned on both sides.

4 Transfer the salmon to a warmed serving dish, then drizzle over some of the sauce and serve hot, garnished with parsley and accompanied by the remaining sauce in a small serving bowl.

Angler Fish, Rosemary & Bacon Skewers

SERVES TWELVE

12 oz/350 g angler fish tail or
  9 oz/250 g angler fish fillet
12 fresh rosemary stems
3 tbsp Spanish olive oil
juice of ½ small lemon
1 garlic clove, crushed
6 thick strips Canadian
  bacon
salt and pepper
lemon wedges, to garnish
Aïoli (see page 12), to serve

1 If using angler fish tail, cut either side of the central bone with a sharp knife and remove the flesh to form 2 fillets. Slice the fillets in half lengthwise, then cut each fillet into 12 bite-size chunks to give a total of 24 pieces. Place the angler fish pieces in a large bowl.

2 To prepare the rosemary skewers, strip the leaves off the stems and reserve them, leaving a few leaves at one end. For the marinade, finely chop the reserved leaves and whisk together in a bowl with the olive oil, lemon juice, garlic, and salt and pepper to taste. Add the angler fish pieces and toss until coated in the marinade. Cover and let marinate in the refrigerator for 1–2 hours.

3 Cut each bacon strip in half lengthwise, then in half widthwise, and roll up each piece. Thread 2 pieces of angler fish alternately with 2 bacon rolls onto the prepared rosemary skewers.

4 Preheat the broiler, grill pan, or grill. If you are cooking the skewers under an overhead broiler, arrange them on the grill pan so that the leaves of the rosemary skewers protrude from the broiler and therefore do not catch fire during cooking. Broil the angler fish and bacon skewers for 10 minutes, turning occasionally and basting with any remaining marinade, or until cooked. Serve hot, garnished with lemon wedges for squeezing over them and accompanied by a small bowl of Aïoli in which to dip the angler fish skewers.

Fried Pickled Angler Fish

SERVES FOUR–SIX

1 lb 5 oz/600 g angler fish tail
2½–3¾ cups olive oil
6 shallots, thinly sliced
2 carrots, sliced
1 fennel bulb, thinly sliced
2 bay leaves
2 garlic cloves, thinly sliced
½ tsp dried chili flakes, or to
   taste
1¼ cups white wine vinegar
salt and pepper
1½ tbsp coriander seeds
fresh flatleaf parsley sprigs,
   to garnish
lemon wedges, to serve

BATTER

1 cup all-purpose flour, plus
   about 4 tbsp extra for
   dusting
½ tsp salt
1 egg, separated
generous ¾ cup beer
1 tbsp olive oil

1 Remove the membrane covering the angler fish, then rinse and pat dry. Cut the tail lengthwise on either side of the central bone, then remove the bone and discard. Cut the fish flesh crosswise into $1/2$-inch/1-cm slices.

2 Heat 4 tablespoons of the olive oil in a skillet over medium heat. Add as many fish slices as will fit in a single layer and cook for 2 minutes. Turn over and cook for 4 minutes, or until the fish flakes easily. Drain on paper towels. Transfer to a nonmetallic bowl and reserve.

3 Heat 1 cup of oil in the skillet. Add the shallots and cook for 3 minutes, or until softened but not browned. Stir in the carrots, fennel, bay leaves, garlic, chili flakes, vinegar, and salt and pepper to taste. Bring to a boil, reduce the heat and simmer for 8 minutes. Stir in the coriander seeds and simmer for 2 minutes, or until the carrots are tender. Pour over the

fish and let stand until cold. Cover and chill for 24 hours and up to 5 days.

4 Make the batter 30 minutes before cooking. Sift the flour and salt into a bowl and make a well in the center. Add the egg yolk and scant $1/2$ cup of the beer and gradually whisk the flour into the liquid until thick. Stir in the oil and enough of the remaining beer to make a thick, smooth batter. Let stand for 30 minutes. Remove the fish from the marinade and pat dry, then reserve. Heat enough olive oil for deep-frying in a large pan until sizzling. Whisk the egg white until stiff peaks form. Stir the batter, then fold in the egg white.

5 Sift the remaining 4 tablespoons of flour onto a plate and season. Roll the fish in it, shaking off the excess flour. Dip the fish in the batter, then deep-fry, in batches, for 3–4 minutes, or until golden. Drain on paper towels. Transfer to a large plate, garnish with parsley, and serve with lemon wedges.

Catalan Fish

SERVES FOUR

4 globe artichokes
2 soles, filleted
½ lemon
1 cup dry white wine
½ stick butter
2 tbsp all-purpose flour
1 cup milk
freshly grated nutmeg
1 bay leaf
2 cups sliced mushrooms
salt and pepper

1 Cut or break off the stems from the artichokes and remove and discard the tough outer leaves. Trim the points of the leaves with kitchen scissors. Place the artichokes in a pan and add enough water to cover and a pinch of salt. Bring to a boil, then reduce the heat and cook for 30 minutes, or until tender.

2 Meanwhile, season the fish fillets to taste with salt and pepper and squeeze over the lemon. Roll up each fillet and secure with a wooden toothpick. Place them in a shallow pan, then pour in the wine and poach gently, spooning over the wine occasionally, for 15 minutes.

3 Melt half the butter in a separate pan, then add the flour and cook, stirring constantly, for 2 minutes, or until golden. Remove the pan from the heat and gradually stir in the milk. Return the pan to the heat and bring to a boil, stirring constantly until thickened and smooth. Reduce the heat to very low, then season to taste with salt, pepper, and nutmeg and add the bay leaf.

4 Melt the remaining butter in a skillet. Add the mushrooms and cook over medium heat, stirring occasionally, for 3 minutes. Remove the skillet from the heat.

5 Remove the artichokes from the pan with a slotted spoon and drain on paper towels. Remove and discard the hairy chokes and prickly leaves. Place the artichokes on serving plates. Divide the mushrooms between the artichoke cavities and spoon in the sauce, removing and discarding the bay leaf. Transfer the fish fillets to a plate with a slotted spoon and remove and discard the toothpicks. Place the fillets in the artichoke cavities and serve.

Broiled Sardines

SERVES FOUR-SIX
12 fresh sardines
2 tbsp garlic-flavored olive oil
coarse sea salt and pepper
lemon wedges, to serve

1 Scrape the scales off the sardines with a knife, then, working with 1 sardine at a time, hold it firmly in one hand and snap off the head with your other hand, pulling downward. This should remove most of the guts with the head, but use a finger to remove any innards that remain. You can then use your thumb and

forefinger to grasp the top of the backbone and pull it toward you to remove. Rinse well and pat dry with paper towels.

2 Preheat the broiler to high and brush the broiler rack with a little of the garlic-flavored olive oil. Brush the sardines with the oil and arrange in a single layer on the broiler rack. Sprinkle with salt and pepper to taste.

3 Broil about 4 inches/10 cm from the heat for 3 minutes, or until the skin becomes crisp. Use kitchen tongs to turn the sardines over and brush with more oil and sprinkle with salt and pepper.

Continue broiling for 2–3 minutes, or until the flesh flakes easily and the skin is crisp. Serve immediately with lemon wedges.

Deep-Fried Sardines

SERVES SIX-EIGHT

⅓ cup red wine vinegar

3 garlic cloves, finely chopped

1 fresh red chili, seeded and
  finely chopped

2 tbsp chopped fresh parsley

2 lb 4 oz/1 kg fresh sardines,
  scaled, cleaned, and heads
  removed (see page 138)

generous ¾ cup all-purpose
  flour

vegetable oil, for deep-frying

salt and pepper

lemon wedges, to garnish

1 Mix the vinegar, garlic, chili, and parsley together in a nonmetallic dish. Add the sardines and turn to coat. Cover with plastic wrap and let marinate in the refrigerator for 1 hour.

2 Drain the sardines and pat dry with paper towels. Place the flour in a plastic bag and season to taste with salt and pepper. Add the sardines, a few at a time, shaking to coat well.

3 Heat the vegetable oil in a deep-fat fryer or large pan to 350–375°F/180–190°C, or until a cube of bread browns in 30 seconds. Deep-fry the sardines, in batches, for 4–5 minutes, or until golden brown. Remove and drain on paper towels. Keep warm while you cook the remaining sardines. Serve garnished with lemon wedges.

Sardines Marinated in Sherry Vinegar

SERVES SIX
12 small fresh sardines
3/4 cup Spanish olive oil
4 tbsp sherry vinegar
2 carrots, cut into julienne
   strips
1 onion, thinly sliced
1 garlic clove, crushed
1 bay leaf
4 tbsp chopped fresh
   flatleaf parsley
salt and pepper
fresh dill sprigs, to garnish
lemon wedges, to serve

1 If it has not already been done, clean the sardines by scraping the scales off with a knife, being careful not to cut the skin. The choice is yours whether you then leave the heads and tails on or cut them off and discard. Slit along the belly of each fish and remove the innards under cold running water. Dry each fish well on paper towels.

2 Heat 4 tablespoons of the olive oil in a large, heavy-bottom skillet. Add the sardines and cook for 10 minutes, or until browned on both sides. Using a spatula, very carefully remove the sardines from the skillet and transfer to a large, shallow, nonmetallic dish that will hold the sardines in a single layer.

3 Gently heat the remaining olive oil and the sherry vinegar in a large pan. Add the carrot strips, onion, garlic, and bay leaf and simmer gently for 5 minutes until softened. Season the vegetables to taste with salt and pepper. Let the mixture cool

slightly, then pour the marinade over the sardines.

4 Cover the dish and let the sardines cool before transferring to the refrigerator. Let marinate for 8 hours or overnight, spooning the marinade over the sardines occasionally. Return the sardines to room temperature before serving, then sprinkle with parsley and garnish with dill sprigs. Serve with lemon wedges.

Sardines with Romesco Sauce

SERVES SIX

24 fresh sardines, scaled,
cleaned, and heads
removed (see page 138)
generous ¾ cup all-purpose
flour
4 eggs, lightly beaten
9 oz/250 g fresh white bread
crumbs
6 tbsp chopped fresh parsley
4 tbsp chopped fresh marjoram
vegetable oil, for deep-frying

ROMESCO SAUCE

1 red bell pepper, halved
and seeded
2 tomatoes, halved
4 garlic cloves
½ cup olive oil
1 slice white bread, diced
4 tbsp blanched almonds
1 fresh red chili, seeded
and chopped
2 shallots, chopped
1 tsp paprika
2 tbsp red wine vinegar
2 tsp sugar
1 tbsp water

1 First make the sauce. Preheat the oven to 425°F/220°C. Place the bell pepper, tomatoes, and garlic in an ovenproof dish and drizzle over 1 tablespoon of the olive oil, turning to coat. Bake in the preheated oven for 20–25 minutes, then remove from the oven and cool. When cool enough to handle, peel off their skins and place the flesh in a food processor.

2 Heat 1 tablespoon of the remaining oil in a skillet. Add the bread and almonds and cook over low heat for a few minutes until browned. Remove and drain on paper towels. Add the chili, shallots, and paprika to the pan and cook for 5 minutes, or until the shallots are softened.

3 Transfer the almond mixture and shallot mixture to the food processor and add the vinegar, sugar, and water. Process to a paste. With the motor still running, gradually add the remaining oil through the feeder tube. Transfer to a bowl, cover, and reserve.

4 Place the sardines, skin-side up, on a cutting board and press along the length of the spines with your thumbs. Turn over and remove and discard the bones. Place the flour and eggs in separate bowls. Mix the bread crumbs and herbs together in a third bowl. Toss the fish in the flour, the eggs, then in the bread crumbs.

5 Heat the vegetable oil in a large pan to 350–375°F/180–190°C, or until a cube of bread browns in 30 seconds. Deep-fry the fish for 4–5 minutes, or until golden and tender. Drain and serve with the sauce.

Sardines with Lemon & Chili

SERVES FOUR

1 lb/450 g fresh sardines, scaled, cleaned, and heads removed

4 tbsp lemon juice

1 garlic clove, finely chopped

1 tbsp finely chopped fresh dill

1 tsp finely chopped fresh red chili

4 tbsp olive oil

salt and pepper

COOK'S TIP: You can serve these sardines, cut into bite-size pieces and speared onto wooden toothpicks, with Picada if you like.

1 Place the sardines, skin-side up, on a cutting board and press along the length of the spines with your thumbs. Turn them over and remove and discard the bones.

2 Place the fillets, skin-side down, in a shallow, nonmetallic dish and sprinkle with the lemon juice. Cover with plastic wrap and let stand in a cool place for 30 minutes.

3 Drain off any excess lemon juice. Sprinkle the garlic, dill, and chili over the fish and season to taste with salt and pepper. Drizzle over the olive oil, then cover with plastic wrap and let chill for 12 hours before serving.

Sardine Escabeche

SERVES SIX

3/4 cup olive oil

2 lb 4 oz/1 kg fresh sardines, scaled, cleaned, and heads removed

3 tbsp red wine vinegar

1/2 tbsp water

4 garlic cloves, peeled

1 bay leaf

2 fresh thyme sprigs

2 fresh rosemary sprigs

4 tbsp chopped fresh parsley

2 fresh red chilies, seeded and chopped

salt and pepper

1 Heat 6 tablespoons of the olive oil in a heavy-bottom skillet. Add the sardines and cook, in batches if necessary, for 4–5 minutes on each side. Remove with a spatula, then drain well and place in a shallow, nonmetallic dish. Cover with plastic wrap and reserve until required.

2 Add the remaining olive oil to the pan and heat gently, then add the vinegar, water, garlic, bay leaf, thyme, rosemary, parsley, and chilies and season to taste with salt and pepper. Bring to a boil, then reduce the heat and let simmer for 15 minutes.

3 Remove the pan from the heat and let cool completely. Pour the mixture over the fish, then cover and let marinate in the refrigerator for at least 24 hours before serving.

Pickled Mackerel

SERVES FOUR-SIX

8 fresh mackerel fillets

1¼ cups extra-virgin olive oil

2 large red onions, thinly sliced

2 carrots, sliced

2 bay leaves

2 garlic cloves, thinly sliced

2 dried red chilies

1 fennel bulb, halved and thinly sliced

1¼ cups sherry vinegar

1½ tbsp coriander seeds

salt and pepper

toasted French bread slices, to serve

1 Preheat the broiler to medium. Place the mackerel fillets, skin-side up, on a broiler rack and brush with oil. Broil under the hot broiler, about 4 inches/10 cm from the heat source, for 4–6 minutes, until the skins become brown and crispy and the flesh flakes easily. Reserve until required.

2 Heat the remaining oil in a large skillet. Add the onions and cook for 5 minutes until softened but not browned. Add the remaining ingredients and let simmer for 10 minutes until the carrots are tender.

3 Flake the mackerel flesh into large pieces, removing the skin and tiny bones. Place the

mackerel pieces in a preserving jar and pour over the onion, carrot, and fennel mixture. (The jar should accommodate everything packed in quite tightly with the minimum air gap at the top once the vegetable mixture has been poured in.) Let cool completely, then cover tightly and let chill for at least 24 hours and up to 5 days. Serve the pieces of mackerel on toasted slices of French bread with a little of the oil drizzled over.

4 Alternatively, serve the mackerel and its pickled vegetables as a first-course salad.

Angulas

SERVES FOUR

3/4 cup olive oil

4 garlic cloves, chopped

1 fresh red chili, seeded and cut into 4 pieces

1 lb 4 oz/550 g baby eels, or cleaned smelts, or whitebait

1 Heat the olive oil in 4 individual, flameproof earthenware dishes. Stir in the garlic and chili.

2 Add the eels and cook, stirring frequently, for a few seconds. If using smelts or whitebait, cook for an additional 2 minutes.

3 As soon as the dishes are sizzling hot, serve immediately.

Tuna Rolls

SERVES FOUR

3 red bell peppers

½ cup olive oil

2 tbsp lemon juice

5 tbsp red wine vinegar

2 garlic cloves, finely chopped

1 tsp paprika

1 tsp dried chili flakes

2 tsp sugar

2 tbsp salted capers

7 oz/200 g canned tuna in oil,
  drained and flaked

1 Preheat the broiler to high. Place the bell peppers on a baking sheet and cook under the preheated broiler, turning frequently, for 10 minutes, until the skin is blackened and blistered all over. Using tongs, transfer to a plastic bag, then tie the top and let cool.

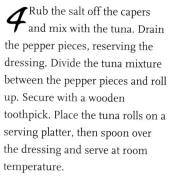

2 Meanwhile, whisk the olive oil, lemon juice, vinegar, garlic, paprika, chili flakes, and sugar together in a small bowl.

3 When the peppers are cool enough to handle, peel off the skins, then cut the flesh into thirds lengthwise and seed. Place the pepper pieces in a nonmetallic dish and pour over the dressing, turning to coat. Let stand in a cool place for 30 minutes.

4 Rub the salt off the capers and mix with the tuna. Drain the pepper pieces, reserving the dressing. Divide the tuna mixture between the pepper pieces and roll up. Secure with a wooden toothpick. Place the tuna rolls on a serving platter, then spoon over the dressing and serve at room temperature.

Tuna, Egg & Potato Salad

SERVES FOUR

12 oz/350 g new potatoes,
    unpeeled
1 hard-cooked egg, cooled
    and shelled
3 tbsp olive oil
1½ tbsp white wine vinegar
4 oz/115 g canned tuna in oil,
    drained and flaked
2 shallots, finely chopped
1 tomato, peeled and diced
2 tbsp chopped fresh parsley
salt and pepper

1 Cook the potatoes in a pan of lightly salted boiling water for 10 minutes, then remove from the heat, cover, and let stand for 15–20 minutes, or until tender.

2 Meanwhile, slice the egg, then cut each slice in half. Whisk the olive oil and vinegar together in a bowl and season to taste with salt and pepper. Spoon a little of the vinaigrette into a serving dish to coat the base.

4 Finally, top the salad with the tomato and parsley. Cover with plastic wrap and let stand in a cool place for 1–2 hours before serving.

3 Drain the potatoes, then peel and thinly slice. Place half the slices over the base of the dish and season to taste with salt, then top with half the tuna, half the egg slices, and half the shallots. Pour over half the remaining dressing. Make a second layer with the remaining potato slices, tuna, egg, and shallots, then pour over the remaining dressing.

Tuna with Pimiento-Stuffed Olives

SERVES SIX

2 fresh tuna steaks,
  weighing about 9 oz/250 g
  in total and about
  1 inch/2.5 cm thick
5 tbsp Spanish olive oil
3 tbsp red wine vinegar
4 fresh thyme sprigs, plus
  extra to garnish
1 bay leaf
2 tbsp all-purpose flour
1 onion, finely chopped
2 garlic cloves, finely chopped
1/2 cup pimiento-stuffed
  green olives, sliced
salt and pepper
crusty bread, to serve

1 Don't get caught out with this recipe—the tuna steaks need to be marinated, so remember to start preparing the dish the day before you are going to serve it. Remove the skin from the tuna steaks, then cut the steaks in half along the grain of the fish. Cut each half into 1/2-inch/1-cm thick slices against the grain.

2 Place 3 tablespoons of the olive oil and the vinegar in a large, shallow, nonmetallic dish. Strip the leaves from the thyme sprigs and add these to the dish with the bay leaf and salt and pepper to taste. Add the prepared strips of tuna, then cover the dish and let marinate in the refrigerator for 8 hours or overnight.

3 The next day, place the flour in a plastic bag. Remove the tuna strips from the marinade, reserving the marinade for later, then add them to the bag of flour and toss well until they are lightly coated in the flour.

4 Heat the remaining olive oil in a large, heavy-bottom skillet. Add the onion and garlic and gently cook for 5–10 minutes, or until softened and golden brown. Add the tuna strips to the skillet and cook for 2–5 minutes, turning several times, until the fish becomes opaque. Add the reserved marinade and olives to the skillet and cook for an additional 1–2 minutes, stirring, until the fish is tender and the sauce has thickened.

5 Serve the tuna and olives piping hot, garnished with fresh thyme sprigs. Accompany with chunks or slices of crusty bread for mopping up the sauce.

Spicy Deep-Fried Whitebait

SERVES FOUR

generous ¾ cup all-purpose
   flour
½ tsp cayenne pepper
½ tsp ground cumin
1 tsp paprika
pinch of salt
2 lb 12 oz/1.25 kg whitebait
vegetable oil, for deep-frying
lemon slices, to garnish

1 Mix the flour, cayenne, cumin, paprika, and salt together in a large bowl, plate, or tray.

2 Rinse the fish and pat dry with paper towels. Add the fish to the seasoned flour, a few at a time, tossing well to coat.

3 Heat the vegetable oil in a deep-fat fryer or large pan to 350–375°F/180–190°C, or until a cube of bread browns in 30 seconds. Deep-fry the fish, in batches, for 2–3 minutes, or until golden brown.

4 Drain well on paper towels and keep warm while you cook the remaining batches. Serve on warmed serving plates, garnished with lemon slices.

Calamari

SERVES SIX

1 lb/450 g prepared squid
all-purpose flour, for coating
corn oil, for deep-frying
salt
lemon wedges, to garnish
Aïoli (see page 12), to serve

1 Slice the squid into 1/2-inch/ 1-cm rings and halve the tentacles if large. Rinse and dry well on paper towels so that they do not spit during cooking. Dust the squid rings with flour so that they are lightly coated. Do not season the flour, as Spanish cooks will tell you that seasoning squid with salt before cooking toughens it.

2 Heat the corn oil in a deep-fat fryer to 350–375°F/180–190°C, or until a cube of bread browns in 30 seconds. Carefully add the squid rings, in batches so that the temperature of the oil does not drop, and deep-fry for 2–3 minutes, or until golden brown and crisp all over, turning several times. Do not overcook, as the squid will become tough and rubbery rather than moist and tender.

3 Using a slotted spoon, remove the fried squid from the deep-fat fryer and drain well on paper towels. Keep warm in a warm oven while you deep-fry the remaining squid rings.

4 Sprinkle the deep-fried squid rings with salt and serve piping hot, garnished with lemon wedges for squeezing over them. Accompany with a small bowl of Aïoli in which to dip the calamari.

Squid & Cherry Tomatoes

SERVES SIX

1 lb 2 oz/500 g prepared squid

scant ⅓ cup olive oil

2 tbsp lemon juice

1 garlic clove, finely chopped

2 tbsp chopped fresh parsley

1 tbsp chopped fresh
  marjoram

pinch of cayenne pepper

1 zucchini

1 bunch of arugula,
  separated into leaves

12 oz/350 g cherry tomatoes

1 Cut the squid into rings ½ inch/1 cm thick. Heat 2 tablespoons of the olive oil in a large, heavy-bottom skillet. Add the squid rings and cook over high heat, stirring constantly, for 3 minutes, or until the flesh becomes opaque and feels tender when pierced with the point of a sharp knife. Using a slotted spoon, transfer the squid to a nonmetallic bowl.

2 Whisk the remaining oil, the lemon juice, garlic, parsley, marjoram, and cayenne together in a bowl, then pour the dressing over the squid. Toss well to coat, cover with plastic wrap, and let cool. Chill for up to 8 hours.

3 Using a swivel-bladed vegetable peeler, cut the zucchini into long ribbons. Combine the zucchini ribbons, arugula leaves, and tomatoes in a dish. Add the squid, together with the dressing, and serve.

Stuffed Squid in their Own Ink

SERVES SIX-EIGHT

60 baby squid or 30 medium
   squid
2/3 cup olive oil
scant 1/2 cup white wine
4 Spanish onions, chopped
1 garlic bulb, separated into
   cloves and peeled
2 green bell peppers, seeded
   and chopped
2 tomatoes, thinly sliced
scant 1/2 cup red wine
scant 1/2 cup water
salt and pepper
snipped fresh chives,
   to garnish

1 Partially fill a bowl with cold water. Clean each squid by gently pulling off the head. The insides will come away at the same time. Remove and reserve the ink sacs in the bowl of water. Cut off the tentacles from the heads, squeeze out and discard the beaks, scrape off the suckers with a sharp knife, then chop. Rinse the bodies and rub off the skin. Stuff the body sacs with the tentacles.

2 Heat 4 tablespoons of the olive oil in a large, heavy-bottom skillet. Season the squid to taste with salt. Add to the pan, then cover and cook, in batches if necessary, over low heat, turning occasionally, for 5 minutes, or until golden brown all over. Drain well and reserve. Add more oil to the skillet as required.

3 Pour the bowl of ink sacs into a food processor or blender, then add the white wine and process until combined. Reserve.

4 Heat 4 tablespoons of the remaining oil in a separate skillet. Add the onions and cook over low heat, stirring occasionally, for 5 minutes. Add the garlic and green bell peppers, then cover and cook for 15–20 minutes, or until the vegetables are very soft but not browned. Stir in the tomatoes, then pour in the ink mixture. Transfer the contents of the pan to the food processor or blender.

5 Add the squid to the skillet, turning to coat in the mixture remaining on the bottom of the skillet, then transfer to a flameproof casserole. Pour the red wine into the skillet, then add the water and cook over low heat, scraping up the sediment from the bottom of the skillet with a wooden spoon. Pour this mixture into the food processor or blender and process until combined. Press the sauce through a strainer, then pour it over the squid.

6 Cover the casserole dish and cook the squid in the sauce over low heat for 1 hour. Serve immediately, sprinkled with the chives, or set aside until required and reheat gently before serving.

Squid & Beans

SERVES SIX

1 lb 2 oz/500 g prepared squid
3 garlic cloves, chopped
1¼ cups dry red wine
1 lb 2 oz/500 g new potatoes,
 unpeeled
225 g/8 oz green beans,
 cut into short lengths
4 tbsp olive oil
1 tbsp red wine vinegar
salt and pepper

1 Preheat the oven to 350°F/180°C. Using a sharp knife, cut the squid into rings about ¹/2 inch/1 cm thick and place them in an ovenproof dish. Sprinkle with half the garlic, then pour over the wine and season to taste with salt and pepper. Cover the dish with foil and bake in the preheated oven for 45–50 minutes, or until the squid feels tender when pierced with the point of a sharp knife.

2 Meanwhile, cook the potatoes in a pan of lightly salted boiling water for 15–20 minutes, or until tender. Drain and let cool slightly, then thickly slice and place in a large bowl.

3 Cook the beans in a separate pan of lightly salted boiling water for 3–5 minutes, or until tender. Drain and add to the potatoes. Drain the squid and add to the bowl.

4 Whisk the olive oil, vinegar, and remaining garlic together in a bowl and season to taste with salt and pepper. Pour the dressing over the salad and toss lightly. Divide the salad between individual serving plates and serve warm.

Crab with Almonds

SERVES FOUR

1 lb/450 g fresh, canned, or
  frozen crabmeat, thawed
1 stick butter
3 oz/85 g slivered almonds
1/2 cup heavy cream
1 tbsp chopped fresh parsley
salt and pepper

1 Pick over the crabmeat to remove any pieces of cartilage or shell. Melt half the butter in a heavy-bottom skillet. Add the crabmeat and cook over medium heat, stirring occasionally, for 10 minutes, or until browned. Remove the skillet from the heat and reserve.

2 Melt the remaining butter in a separate skillet. Add the almonds and cook over low heat, stirring occasionally, for 5 minutes, or until golden brown.

3 Stir the almonds into the crabmeat and season to taste with salt and pepper. Stir in the cream and parsley and bring to a boil. Reduce the heat and simmer for 3 minutes. Transfer to a warmed serving dish and serve immediately.

Crab Tartlets

MAKES TWENTY-FOUR

1 tbsp Spanish olive oil
1 small onion, finely chopped
1 garlic clove, finely chopped
splash of dry white wine
2 eggs
2/3 cup milk or light cream
6 oz/175 g canned crabmeat,
   drained
2 oz/55 g Manchego or
   Parmesan cheese, grated
2 tbsp chopped fresh
   flatleaf parsley
pinch of freshly grated
   nutmeg
salt and pepper
fresh dill sprigs, to garnish

PASTRY

2 1/3 cups all-purpose flour, plus
   extra for dusting
pinch of salt
1 1/2 sticks butter
2 tbsp cold water
OR
1 lb 2 oz/500 g ready-made
   unsweetened pastry

1 Preheat the oven to 375°F/190°C. To prepare the crabmeat filling, heat the olive oil in a pan. Add the onion and cook for 5 minutes, or until softened but not browned. Add the garlic and cook for an additional 30 seconds. Add a splash of white wine and cook for 1–2 minutes, or until most of the wine has evaporated.

2 Lightly whisk the eggs in a large bowl, then whisk in the milk or cream. Add the crabmeat, grated cheese, parsley, and the onion mixture. Season the mixture with nutmeg and salt and pepper to taste and mix together.

3 To prepare the pastry if you are making it yourself, mix the flour and salt together in a large bowl. Add the butter, cut into small pieces, and rub it in until the mixture resembles fine bread crumbs. Gradually stir in enough of the water to form a firm dough. Alternatively, the pastry could be made in a food processor.

4 Thinly roll out the pastry on a lightly floured counter. Using a plain, round 2 3/4-inch/7-cm cutter, cut the pastry into 18 circles. Gently pile the trimmings together and roll out again, then cut out an additional 6 circles. Use to line 24 x 1 1/2-inch/4-cm tartlet pans. Carefully spoon the crabmeat mixture into the pastry shells, taking care not to overfill them.

5 Bake the tartlets in the preheated oven for 25–30 minutes, or until golden brown and set. Serve the crab tartlets hot or cold, garnished with fresh dill sprigs.

Sweet Peppers Stuffed with Crab Salad

MAKES SIXTEEN

16 pimientos del piquillo, drained, or freshly roasted sweet peppers, tops cut off

chopped fresh parsley, to garnish

CRAB SALAD

8½ oz/240 g canned crabmeat, drained and squeezed dry

1 red bell pepper, broiled, peeled (see page 74), and chopped

about 2 tbsp fresh lemon juice

scant 1 cup cream cheese

salt and pepper

1 First make the crab salad. Pick over the crabmeat and remove any bits of shell. Put half the crabmeat in a food processor with the prepared red bell pepper, 1¹/2 tablespoons of the lemon juice, and salt and pepper to taste. Process until well blended, then transfer to a bowl. Flake and stir in the cream cheese and remaining crabmeat. Taste and add extra lemon juice, if required.

2 Pat the pimientos del piquillo dry and scoop out any seeds that remain in the tips. Use a small spoon to divide the crab salad equally between the pimientos, stuffing them generously. Arrange on a large serving dish or individual plates, then cover and let chill until required. Just before serving, sprinkle the stuffed pimientos with the chopped parsley.

COOK'S TIP: If you can't find pimientos del piquillo, and have to roast the peppers yourself, use 16 of the long, sweet Mediterranean variety, not capsicums. If, however, capsicums are the only ones you can find, cut 4-6 into wedges and spread the crab salad along each wedge.

Battered Shrimp & Cilantro Dip

SERVES FOUR

12 raw Mediterranean shrimp

1 egg

1/2 cup water

generous 3/4 cup all-purpose flour

1 tsp cayenne pepper

vegetable oil, for deep-frying

orange wedges, to garnish

CILANTRO DIP

1 large bunch of cilantro, coarsely chopped

3 garlic cloves, chopped

2 tbsp tomato paste

2 tbsp lemon juice

1 tbsp grated lemon rind

1 1/2 tbsp sugar

1 tsp ground cumin

5 tbsp olive oil

1 First make the cilantro dip. Place the cilantro, garlic, tomato paste, lemon juice, lemon rind, sugar, and cumin in a food processor or blender and process until combined. With the motor still running, gradually add the olive oil through the feeder tube until fully incorporated. Scrape into a bowl, then cover with plastic wrap and let chill until required.

2 Pull the heads off the shrimp and peel, leaving the tails intact. Cut along the length of the back of each shrimp and remove and discard the dark vein. Rinse under cold running water, then pat dry with paper towels.

3 Whisk the egg with the water in a small bowl. Gradually sift in the flour and cayenne, whisking constantly until smooth.

4 Heat the vegetable oil in a deep-fat fryer or large pan to 350–375°F/180–190°C, or until a cube of bread browns in 30 seconds. Holding the shrimp by their tails, dip them into the batter, one at a time, shaking off any excess. Add the shrimp to the oil and deep-fry for 2–3 minutes, or until crisp. Remove with a slotted spoon and drain well on paper towels. Serve immediately, garnished with orange wedges. Hand round the cilantro dip separately.

Garlic Shrimp with Lemon and Parsley

SERVES SIX

60 raw jumbo shrimp, thawed
   if using frozen
⅔ cup olive oil
6 garlic cloves, thinly sliced
3 dried hot red chilies
   (optional)
6 tbsp freshly squeezed lemon
   juice
6 tbsp very finely chopped
   fresh parsley
French bread, to serve

1 Peel and devein the shrimp and remove the heads, leaving the tails on. Rinse and pat the shrimp dry.

2 Heat the olive oil in a large, deep sauté pan or skillet. Add the garlic and chilies, if using, and stir constantly until they begin to sizzle. Add the shrimp and cook until they turn pink and begin to curl.

3 Use a slotted spoon to transfer the shrimp to warm earthenware bowls. Sprinkle each bowl with lemon juice and parsley. Serve with plenty of bread to mop up the juices.

Giant Garlic Shrimp

SERVES FOUR

⅓ cup olive oil

4 garlic cloves, finely chopped

2 hot fresh red chilies,
  seeded and finely chopped

1 lb/450 g cooked jumbo
  shrimp

2 tbsp chopped fresh
  flatleaf parsley

salt and pepper

lemon wedges, to garnish

crusty bread, to serve

1 Heat the olive oil in a preheated wok or large, heavy-bottom skillet over low heat. Add the garlic and chilies and cook, stirring occasionally, for 1–2 minutes, until softened but not colored.

2 Add the shrimp and stir-fry for 2–3 minutes, or until heated through and coated in the oil and garlic mixture.

3 Turn off the heat and add the chopped parsley, stirring well to mix. Season to taste with salt and pepper.

4 Divide the shrimp and garlic-flavored oil between warmed serving dishes and garnish with lemon wedges. Serve with lots of crusty bread.

Lime-Drizzled Shrimp

SERVES SIX

4 limes
12 raw jumbo shrimp,
  in their shells
3 tbsp Spanish olive oil
2 garlic cloves, finely chopped
splash of dry sherry
4 tbsp chopped fresh
  flatleaf parsley
salt and pepper

1 Grate the rind and squeeze out the juice from 2 of the limes. Cut the remaining 2 limes into wedges and reserve until required.

2 To prepare the shrimp, remove the legs, leaving the shells and tails intact. Cut along the length of the back of each shrimp and remove the dark vein and discard. Rinse the shrimp under cold running water and dry well on paper towels.

3 Heat the oil in a large, heavy-bottom skillet, then add the garlic and cook for 30 seconds. Add the shrimp and cook for 5 minutes, stirring occasionally, or until they turn pink and begin to curl. Mix in the lime rind, juice, and a splash of sherry to moisten, then stir well together.

4 Transfer the cooked shrimp to a serving dish, then season to taste with salt and pepper and sprinkle over the chopped parsley.

5 Serve piping hot, accompanied by the reserved lime wedges for squeezing over the shrimp.

Shrimp Wrapped in Ham

MAKES SIXTEEN

16 raw jumbo shrimp

16 thin slices serrano ham
   or prosciutto

extra-virgin olive oil

TOMATO-CAPER DRESSING

2 tomatoes, peeled and
   seeded

1 small red onion, very
   finely chopped

4 tbsp very finely chopped
   fresh parsley

1 tbsp capers in brine,
   drained, rinsed, and
   chopped

finely grated rind of 1 large
   lemon

4 tbsp extra-virgin olive oil

1 tbsp sherry vinegar

COOK'S TIP: To peel and seed tomatoes, remove the stems and cut a cross in the tops. Place them in a heatproof bowl, then pour over boiling water to cover and let stand for 30 seconds. Use a slotted spoon to transfer to a bowl of iced water. Peel off the skins then cut in half and scoop out the cores and seeds.

1 Preheat the oven to 325°F/160°C. To make the dressing, finely chop the prepared tomato flesh and place in a bowl. Add the onion, parsley, capers, and lemon rind and gently toss together. Combine the olive oil and vinegar and add to the other ingredients. Reserve until required.

2 Pull the heads off the shrimp and peel, leaving the tails intact. Cut along the length of the back of each shrimp and remove and discard the dark vein. Rinse and pat dry. Wrap a slice of ham around each shrimp and rub with a little oil. Place the shrimp in a heatproof dish large enough to hold them in a single layer. Bake in the preheated oven for 10 minutes.

3 Transfer the shrimp to a serving platter and spoon the dressing over. Serve immediately, or let cool to room temperature.

Shrimp with Saffron Dressing

SERVES SIX-EIGHT

large pinch of saffron
  threads
2 tbsp warm water
⅔ cup mayonnaise
2 tbsp grated onion
4 tbsp lemon juice
1 tsp Dijon mustard
2 lb 4 oz/1 kg cooked
  Mediterranean shrimp
1 romaine lettuce, separated
  into leaves
4 tomatoes, cut into wedges
8 black olives
salt and pepper

1 Stir the saffron with the water in a small bowl. Mix the mayonnaise, onion, lemon juice, and mustard together in a separate, nonmetallic bowl, whisking gently until thoroughly combined. Season to taste with salt and pepper and stir in the saffron soaking liquid. Cover with plastic wrap and let chill until required.

2 Pull the heads off the shrimp and peel. Cut along the length of the back of each shrimp and remove and discard the dark vein. Rinse and pat dry with paper towels.

3 Arrange the lettuce leaves on a large serving platter or on individual serving plates. Top with the shrimp and scatter with the tomato wedges and olives. Serve with the saffron dressing.

Spicy Shrimp in Sherry

SERVES FOUR

12 raw Mediterranean shrimp
2 tbsp olive oil
2 tbsp dry sherry
pinch of cayenne pepper or
   dash of Tabasco sauce
salt and pepper

1 Pull the heads off the shrimp and peel, leaving the tails intact. Cut along the length of the back of each shrimp and remove and discard the dark vein. Rinse and pat dry.

2 Heat the olive oil in a large, heavy-bottom skillet. Add the shrimp and cook over medium heat, stirring occasionally, for 2–3 minutes, or until they have turned pink. Add the sherry and season to taste with cayenne, salt, and pepper.

3 Tip the contents of the skillet onto a serving platter. Impale each shrimp with a wooden toothpick and serve.

Saffron Shrimp with Lemon Mayonnaise

SERVES SIX-EIGHT

2 lb 12 oz/1.25 kg raw
  Mediterranean shrimp
generous ½ cup all-purpose
  flour
½ cup light beer
2 tbsp olive oil
pinch of saffron powder
2 egg whites
vegetable oil, for deep-frying

LEMON MAYONNAISE

4 garlic cloves
2 egg yolks
1 tbsp lemon juice
1 tbsp finely grated lemon
  rind
1¼ cups corn oil
sea salt and pepper

1 First make the mayonnaise. Place the garlic cloves on a cutting board and sprinkle with a little sea salt, then flatten them with the side of a heavy knife. Finely chop and flatten again.

2 Transfer the garlic to a food processor or blender and add the egg yolks, lemon juice, and lemon rind. Process briefly until just blended. With the motor still running, gradually add the corn oil through the feeder tube until it is fully incorporated. Scrape the mayonnaise into a serving bowl and season to taste with salt and pepper, then cover and let chill until required.

3 Pull the heads off the shrimp and peel, leaving the tails intact. Cut along the length of the back of each shrimp and remove and discard the dark vein. Rinse under cold running water and pat dry with paper towels.

4 Sift the flour into a bowl. Mix the beer, oil, and saffron together in a pitcher, then gradually whisk into the flour. Cover and let stand at room temperature for 30 minutes to rest.

5 Whisk the egg whites in a spotlessly clean, greasefree bowl until stiff. Gently fold the egg whites into the flour mixture.

6 Heat the vegetable oil in a deep-fat fryer or large pan to 350–375°F/180–190°C, or until a cube of bread browns in 30 seconds. Holding the shrimp by their tails, dip them into the batter and shake off any excess. Add the shrimp to the oil and deep-fry for 2–3 minutes, or until crisp. Remove with a slotted spoon and drain well on paper towels. Serve immediately with the mayonnaise.

Shrimp Rissoles

SERVES EIGHT-TEN

1¾ cups all-purpose flour, plus
    extra for dusting
2¼ sticks butter
⅔ cup ice water
1 tsp lemon juice
1 cup milk
freshly grated nutmeg
1 bay leaf
1 lb/450 g cooked shelled
    shrimp
1 hard-cooked egg, cooled,
    shelled, and chopped
1 tbsp paprika
pinch of cayenne pepper
1 tbsp chopped fresh parsley
vegetable oil, for deep-frying
salt and pepper

1 Sift 1 ¹/2 cups of the flour with a pinch of salt into a bowl. Add ¹/2 stick of the butter and rub it in until the mixture resembles bread crumbs. Stir in the water and lemon juice and mix to a dough. Knead lightly and shape into a ball, then cover and chill for 15 minutes. Place 1 ¹/2 sticks of the remaining butter between 2 sheets of waxed paper and beat out into a rectangle ¹/4 inch/5 mm thick.

2 Roll out the dough on a lightly floured counter into a rectangle ¹/4 inch/5 mm thick. Place the butter rectangle in the center. Fold the top and bottom of the dough over it, then wrap in foil and let the package chill for 10 minutes.

3 Place the dough on a lightly floured counter with a folded edge facing you. Roll out to about ¹/4 inch/5 mm thick, then fold into 3 again. Wrap and let chill for 15 minutes. Repeat rolling and folding twice more.

4 Meanwhile, melt the remaining butter in a pan. Add the remaining flour and cook, stirring constantly, for 2 minutes, or until golden. Remove from the heat and gradually stir in the milk. Return to the heat and bring to a

boil, stirring constantly until thickened and smooth. Reduce the heat to very low and season to taste with salt, pepper, and nutmeg, and add the bay leaf. Remove from the heat and let cool.

5 Mix the shrimp and egg together in a bowl, then fold in the sauce, removing the bay leaf. Stir in the paprika, cayenne, and parsley.

6 Roll out the dough to a rectangle about ¹/4 inch/5 mm thick and cut into 3-inch/7.5-cm squares. Place 1 teaspoon of the shrimp mixture on each square. Brush the edges with water and fold the dough over to make triangles, pressing the edges to seal.

7 Heat the vegetable oil in a deep-fat fryer or large pan to 350–375°F/180–190°C, or until a cube of bread browns in 30 seconds. Deep-fry the dough triangles, in batches, for 2 minutes, or until golden and puffed up. Remove with a slotted spoon and drain on paper towels. Serve hot.

Sizzling Chili Shrimp

SERVES SIX

1 lb 2 oz/500 g raw jumbo
   shrimp, in their shells
1 small fresh red chili
6 tbsp Spanish olive oil
2 garlic cloves, finely chopped
pinch of paprika
salt
crusty bread, to serve

1 Pull the heads off the shrimp and peel, leaving the tails intact. Cut along the length of the back of each shrimp and remove and discard the dark vein. Rinse the shrimp under cold running water and pat dry on paper towels.

2 Cut the chili in half lengthwise, then remove the seeds and finely chop the flesh.

3 Heat the oil in a large, heavy-bottom skillet or flameproof casserole until quite hot, then add the garlic and cook for 30 seconds. Add the shrimp, chili, paprika, and a pinch of salt and cook for 2–3 minutes, stirring constantly, until the shrimp turn pink and begin to curl.

4 Serve the shrimp in the cooking dish, still sizzling. Accompany with wooden toothpicks, to spear the shrimp, and chunks or slices of crusty bread to mop up the aromatic cooking oil.

Cidered Scallops

SERVES FOUR-FIVE

4 cups dry cider
4 tbsp lemon juice
20 shelled scallops
3/4 stick butter
2 tbsp all-purpose flour
1 cup sour cream
4 oz/115 g white mushrooms
salt and pepper

1 Preheat the oven to 225°F/110°C. Pour the cider and lemon juice into a large, shallow pan and season to taste with salt and pepper. Add the scallops and poach for 10 minutes, or until tender. Using a slotted spoon, transfer the scallops to an ovenproof dish. Dot with 2 tablespoons of the butter, then cover with foil and keep warm in the oven.

2 Bring the scallop cooking liquid to a boil and continue to boil until reduced by about half. Mix together 2 tablespoons of the remaining butter and the flour, mashing well with a fork to make a paste. Beat the paste, a little at a time, into the liquid until thickened and smooth. Stir in the sour cream and simmer gently for 5–10 minutes.

3 Taste the sauce and adjust the seasoning if necessary. Remove the scallops from the oven and return them to the pan, then heat through for 2–3 minutes.

4 Meanwhile, melt the remaining butter in a small skillet. Add the mushrooms and cook over low heat, stirring frequently, for 2–3 minutes. Add them to the pan of scallops, then transfer to individual serving dishes and serve.

Scallops with Serrano Ham

SERVES FOUR

2 tbsp lemon juice

3 tbsp olive oil

2 garlic cloves, finely chopped

1 tbsp chopped fresh parsley

12 shelled scallops, preferably
  with corals

16 wafer-thin slices serrano
  ham

pepper

1 Mix the lemon juice, olive oil, garlic, and parsley together in a nonmetallic dish. Separate the corals, if using, from the scallops and add both to the dish, turning to coat. Cover with plastic wrap and let marinate at room temperature for 20 minutes.

2 Preheat the broiler to medium. Drain the scallops, reserving the marinade. Scrunch up a slice of ham and thread it onto a metal skewer, followed by a scallop and a coral, if using. Repeat to fill 4 skewers each with the ham, scallops, and corals, finishing with a scrunched-up slice of ham.

3 Cook under the hot broiler, basting with the marinade and turning frequently, for 5 minutes, or until the scallops are tender and the ham is crisp.

4 Transfer to warmed serving plates and sprinkle them with pepper. Spoon over the cooking juices from the broiler pan and serve.

Seared Scallops

SERVES FOUR-SIX
4 tbsp olive oil

3 tbsp orange juice

2 tsp hazelnut oil

24 shelled scallops

salad greens (optional)

6 oz/175 g Cabrales or other
blue cheese, crumbled

2 tbsp chopped fresh dill

salt and pepper

1 Whisk 3 tablespoons of the olive oil, the orange juice, and hazelnut oil together in a pitcher and season to taste with salt and pepper.

2 Heat the remaining olive oil in a large, heavy-bottom skillet. Add the scallops and cook over high heat for 1 minute on each side, or until golden.

3 Transfer the scallops to a bed of salad greens or individual plates. Scatter over the cheese and dill, then drizzle with the dressing. Serve warm.

Scallops in Orange Juice

SERVES SIX

all-purpose flour, for dusting

30 shelled scallops, preferably
   with corals

4 tbsp olive oil

scant ⅓ cup freshly
   squeezed orange juice

salt and pepper

fresh parsley sprigs,
   to garnish

1 Spread out the flour on a
shallow plate. Add the scallops,
a few at a time, and turn to coat
well. Shake off any excess flour.

2 Heat the olive oil in a large,
heavy-bottom skillet. Add the
scallops and cook, turning once,
for 2 minutes, or until tender.
Season to taste with salt and pepper,
then add the orange juice and cook
for an additional 2 minutes.

3 Transfer to warmed serving
plates and serve immediately,
garnished with parsley sprigs.

Scallops in Saffron Sauce

SERVES EIGHT

⅔ cup dry white wine
⅔ cup fish stock
large pinch of saffron
   threads
2 lb/900 g shelled scallops,
   preferably large ones
3 tbsp Spanish olive oil
1 small onion, finely chopped
2 garlic cloves, finely chopped
⅔ cup heavy cream
squeeze of lemon juice
salt and pepper
chopped fresh flatleaf
   parsley plus extra sprigs
   to garnish
crusty bread, to serve

1 Place the wine, fish stock, and saffron in a pan and bring to a boil. Reduce the heat, then cover and simmer gently for 15 minutes.

2 Meanwhile, remove and discard from each scallop the tough, white muscle that is found opposite the coral, and separate the coral from the scallop. Slice the scallops vertically into thick slices,

including the corals if they are present. Dry the scallops well on paper towels, then season to taste.

3 Heat the olive oil in a large, heavy-bottom skillet. Add the onion and garlic and cook for 5 minutes, or until softened and lightly browned. Add the sliced scallops to the pan and cook gently for 5 minutes, stirring occasionally, or until they just turn opaque. The secret is not to overcook the scallops, otherwise they will become tough and rubbery.

4 Using a slotted spoon, remove the scallops from the skillet and transfer to a warmed

plate. Add the saffron liquid to the pan, then bring to a boil and boil rapidly until reduced to about half. Reduce the heat and gradually stir in the cream, just a little at a time. Simmer gently until the sauce thickens.

5 Return the scallops to the skillet and simmer for 1–2 minutes just to heat them through. Add a squeeze of lemon juice and season to taste with salt and pepper. Serve the scallops hot, garnished with the parsley and accompanied by chunks or slices of crusty bread to mop up the saffron sauce.

Baked Scallops

SERVES FOUR

1 lb 9 oz/700 g shelled
   scallops, chopped
2 onions, finely chopped
2 garlic cloves, finely chopped
3 tbsp chopped fresh parsley
pinch of freshly grated
   nutmeg
pinch of ground cloves
2 tbsp fresh white bread
   crumbs
2 tbsp olive oil
salt and pepper

1 Preheat the oven to 400°F/200°C. Mix the scallops, onions, garlic, 2 tablespoons of the parsley, the nutmeg, and cloves together in a bowl and season to taste with salt and pepper.

2 Divide the mixture between 4 scrubbed scallop shells or heatproof dishes. Sprinkle the bread crumbs and remaining parsley on top and drizzle with the olive oil.

3 Bake the scallops in the preheated oven for 15–20 minutes, or until lightly golden and piping hot. Serve immediately.

Catalan Mussels

SERVES FOUR

4 lb 8 oz/2 kg live mussels, scrubbed and debearded
5 tbsp olive oil
2 onions, chopped
2 garlic cloves, finely chopped
4 large tomatoes, peeled, seeded (see page 167), and finely chopped
1 bay leaf
1 tbsp brandy
1/2 tsp paprika
salt and pepper
crusty bread, to serve

1 Discard any mussels with broken or damaged shells and any that do not shut immediately when sharply tapped with the back of a knife.

2 Heat the olive oil in a large, heavy-bottom pan or flameproof casserole. Add the onion and garlic and cook over low heat, stirring occasionally, for 5 minutes, or until softened. Add the tomatoes and bay leaf and cook, stirring occasionally, for an additional 5 minutes.

3 Stir in the brandy and paprika and season to taste with salt and pepper. Increase the heat and add the mussels, then cover the pan and cook, shaking the pan occasionally, for 5 minutes, or until the shells have opened. Discard the bay leaf and any mussels that have not opened. Transfer the mussels to a warmed serving dish and pour the sauce over them. Serve immediately with crusty bread or let cool.

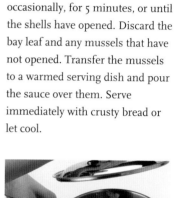

Golden Mussels

SERVES FOUR-SIX

1 lb 2 oz/500 g live mussels
about ¾ cup water
4 tbsp olive oil
1 garlic clove, finely chopped
2 tbsp chopped fresh parsley
¾ cup fresh white bread
    crumbs
1 tomato, peeled,
    seeded (see page 167),
    and chopped

1 Scrub the mussels under cold running water and pull out any beards that are attached to them. Discard any mussels with broken shells or any that do not close immediately when sharply tapped with the back of a knife.

2 Place the mussels in a large pan and add the water. Bring to a boil, then cover and cook over high heat, shaking the pan occasionally, for 3–5 minutes, or until the mussels have opened. Discard any that remain closed.

3 Discard the empty half-shells. Remove the mussels from the other half-shells. Reserving these

shells, mix the mussels, olive oil, garlic, and parsley together in a bowl. Cover with plastic wrap and chill for 30 minutes.

4 Preheat the oven to 425°F/220°C. Mix the bread crumbs and tomato together in a separate bowl. Return the mussels to the reserved half-shells and place in an ovenproof dish in a single layer. Spoon the bread-crumb mixture over the mussels and bake in the preheated oven for 5 minutes, or until hot and golden brown. Serve immediately.

Chili-Marinated Mussels

SERVES SIX-EIGHT

2 lb 4 oz/1 kg live mussels

1 lemon, sliced

2 garlic cloves, finely chopped

3/4 cup white wine

1/2 cup olive oil

3 tbsp lemon juice

1 tbsp Dijon mustard

2 tsp sugar

1 fresh red chili, seeded and
  finely chopped

2 tbsp chopped fresh parsley

1 tbsp capers in brine, drained
  and chopped

rock salt or crushed ice, to
  serve (optional)

1 Scrub the mussels under cold running water and pull out any beards that are attached to them. Discard any mussels with broken shells or any that do not close immediately when sharply tapped with the back of a knife.

2 Place the lemon slices and garlic in a large, heavy-bottom pan, then pour in the wine and bring to a boil. Add the mussels, then cover and cook over high heat, shaking the pan occasionally, for 3–5 minutes, or until the mussels have opened. Discard any that remain closed.

3 Discard the empty half-shells. Remove the mussels from the other half-shells, reserving these half-shells. Mix the olive oil, lemon juice, mustard, sugar, chili, parsley, and capers together in a large, nonmetallic bowl. Add the mussels and toss well to coat. Cover with plastic wrap and let marinate in the refrigerator for up to 24 hours.

4 To serve, return the mussels to the reserved half-shells and arrange on a bed of rock salt or crushed ice on a serving platter, if you like. Spoon the marinade over the mussels and serve.

Mussels with Garlic Butter

SERVES EIGHT

1 lb 12 oz/800 g live mussels,
   in their shells
splash of dry white wine
1 bay leaf
3/4 stick butter
12 oz/350 g fresh white or
   brown bread crumbs
4 tbsp chopped fresh
   flatleaf parsley, plus extra
   sprigs to garnish
2 tbsp snipped fresh chives
2 garlic cloves, finely chopped
salt and pepper
lemon wedges, to serve

1 Clean the mussels by scrubbing or scraping the shells and pulling out any beards that are attached to them. Discard any with broken shells and any that refuse to close when sharply tapped with the back of a knife. Place the mussels in a colander and rinse under cold running water.

2 Place the mussels in a large pan and add a splash of wine and the bay leaf. Cook, covered, over high heat for 5 minutes, shaking the pan occasionally, or until the mussels are opened. Drain the mussels and discard any that remain closed.

3 Shell the mussels, reserving one half of each shell. Arrange the mussels, in their half-shells, in a large, shallow, ovenproof serving dish.

4 Melt the butter and pour into a bowl. Add the bread crumbs, parsley, chives, and garlic and season to taste, then mix well together. Let stand until the butter has set slightly. Using your fingers or 2 teaspoons, take a large pinch of the herb and butter mixture and use to fill each mussel shell, pressing it down well. Let the mussels chill until ready to serve.

5 To serve, preheat the oven to 450°F/230°C. Bake the mussels in the preheated oven for 10 minutes, or until hot. Serve immediately, garnished with parsley sprigs and accompanied by lemon wedges for squeezing over them.

Deep-Fried Mussels with A Chili Dressing

SERVES SIX-EIGHT

4 tbsp olive oil
2 tbsp white wine vinegar
1 tbsp chopped fresh parsley
1-2 fresh red chilies, seeded
    and finely chopped
1 fresh green chili, seeded
    and finely chopped
½ tsp sugar
2 lb 4 oz/1 kg live mussels
about ¾ cup water
2 oz/55 g instant polenta
vegetable oil, for deep-frying

1 Mix the olive oil, vinegar, parsley, chilies, and sugar together in a bowl. Cover with plastic wrap and let chill until required.

2 Scrub the mussels under cold running water and pull out any beards that are attached to them. Discard any mussels with broken shells or any that do not close immediately when sharply tapped with the back of a knife.

3 Place the mussels in a large pan and add the water. Bring to a boil, then cover and cook over high heat, shaking the pan occasionally, for 3–5 minutes, or until the mussels have opened.

Discard any that remain closed.

4 Remove the mussels from the shells, discarding the shells. Spread out the polenta on a shallow plate. Toss the mussels, a few at a time, in the polenta to coat, shaking off any excess.

5 Heat the vegetable oil in a deep-fat fryer or large pan to 350–375°F/180–190°C, or until a cube of bread browns in 30 seconds. Deep-fry the mussels, in batches if necessary, for a few minutes until golden brown. Drain on paper towels and serve hot with the dressing.

Mussels with Yellow Bell Pepper Sauce

SERVES FOUR-SIX

½ cucumber, peeled and
   halved lengthwise
2 onions, chopped
2 tbsp chopped fresh parsley
1 yellow bell pepper, seeded
   and chopped
1 fresh red chili, seeded
   and chopped
⅔ cup dry white wine
2 tbsp olive oil
1 tbsp lemon juice
1 lb 2 oz/500 g live mussels
salt and pepper

1 Scoop out the seeds from the cucumber using a teaspoon, then finely chop the flesh. Mix the cucumber, half the onion, half the parsley, the yellow bell pepper, and chili together in a nonmetallic bowl and season to taste with salt and pepper. Whisk in 2 tablespoons of the wine, the olive oil, and lemon juice. Cover with plastic wrap and let stand at room temperature for 30 minutes.

2 Scrub the mussels under cold running water and pull out any beards that are attached to them. Discard any mussels with broken shells or any that do not close immediately when sharply tapped with the back of a knife.

3 Pour the remaining wine into a large, heavy-bottom pan and add the remaining onion and parsley. Bring to a boil and add the mussels. Cover and cook over high heat, shaking the pan occasionally, for 3–5 minutes, or until the mussels have opened. Discard any that remain closed.

4 Discard the empty half-shells. Place the mussels, in the remaining half-shells, on serving plates. Spoon the sauce over them and serve.

Almejas a la Plancha

SERVES FOUR-SIX

1 lb 2 oz/500 g fresh
  carpet-shell or other
  medium-size clams
olive oil, for brushing and
  drizzling
lemon wedges, to garnish

1 Scrub the clams under cold running water. Discard any with broken shells or any that do not close immediately when sharply tapped with the back of a knife.

2 Heat a grill pan over high heat, then brush with olive oil. Add the clams in a single layer. As soon as they have opened, turn them over so that they are flesh-side down and cook for 2 minutes.

3 Turn the clams again and drizzle with a little more oil. Transfer to a serving platter and pour over the grill pan juices. Garnish with lemon wedges and serve immediately.

Clams with Fava Beans

SERVES FOUR–SIX

4 canned anchovy fillets
  in oil, drained
1 tsp salted capers
3 tbsp olive oil
1 tbsp sherry vinegar
1 tsp Dijon mustard
1 lb 2 oz/500 g fresh clams
about ¾ cup water
1 lb 2 oz/500 g fava beans,
  shelled if fresh
2 tbsp chopped mixed fresh
  herbs, such as parsley,
  chives, and mint
salt and pepper

1 Place the anchovies in a small bowl, then add water to cover and let soak for 5 minutes. Drain well, then pat dry with paper towels and place in a mortar. Brush the salt off the capers, then add to the mortar and pound to a paste with a pestle.

2 Whisk the olive oil, vinegar, and mustard together in a separate bowl, then whisk in the anchovy paste and season to taste with salt and pepper. Cover with plastic wrap and let stand at room temperature until required.

3 Scrub the clams under cold running water. Discard any with broken shells or any that do not close immediately when sharply tapped with the back of a knife. Place the clams in a large, heavy-bottom pan and add the water. Cover and bring to a boil over high heat. Cook, shaking the pan occasionally, for 3–5 minutes, or until the clams have opened. Discard any that remain closed.

4 Meanwhile, bring a large pan of lightly salted water to a boil. Add the fava beans, then return to a boil and blanch for 5 minutes. Drain, then refresh under cold running water and drain well again. Remove and discard the outer skins and place the fava beans in a bowl.

5 Drain the clams and remove them from their shells. Add to the beans and sprinkle with the herbs. Add the anchovy vinaigrette and toss lightly. Serve warm.

Clams in Tomato & Garlic Sauce

SERVES SIX–EIGHT

2 hard-cooked eggs, cooled, shelled, and halved lengthwise

3 tbsp olive oil

1 Spanish onion, chopped

2 garlic cloves, finely chopped

1 lb 9 oz/700 g tomatoes, peeled and diced

¾ cup fresh white bread crumbs

2 lb 4 oz/1 kg fresh clams

generous 1¾ cups dry white wine

2 tbsp chopped fresh parsley

salt and pepper

lemon wedges, to garnish

1 Scoop out the egg yolks using a teaspoon and rub through a fine strainer into a bowl. Chop the whites and reserve separately.

2 Heat the olive oil in a large, heavy-bottom skillet. Add the onion and cook over low heat, stirring occasionally, for 5 minutes, or until softened. Add the garlic and cook for an additional 3 minutes, then add the tomatoes, bread crumbs, and egg yolks and season to taste with salt and pepper. Cook, stirring occasionally and mashing the mixture with a wooden spoon, for an additional 10–15 minutes, or until thick and pulpy.

3 Meanwhile, scrub the clams under cold running water. Discard any with broken shells or any that do not close immediately when sharply tapped with the back of a knife.

4 Place the clams in a large, heavy-bottom pan. Add the wine and bring to a boil. Cover and cook over high heat, shaking the pan occasionally, for 3–5 minutes, or until the clams have opened. Discard any that remain closed.

5 Using a slotted spoon, transfer the clams to warmed serving bowls. Strain the cooking liquid into the tomato sauce, then stir well and spoon over the clams. Sprinkle with the chopped egg whites and parsley and serve immediately, garnished with lemon wedges.

Oysters with Sherry Vinegar

SERVES FOUR

1 shallot, finely chopped

3 tbsp sherry vinegar

3 tbsp red wine vinegar

1 tbsp sugar

24 fresh oysters

rock salt or crushed ice,
    to serve (optional)

pepper

1 Mix the shallot, vinegars, and sugar together in a nonmetallic bowl and season well with pepper. Cover with plastic wrap and let stand at room temperature for at least 15 minutes so that the flavors mingle.

2 Meanwhile, shuck the oysters. Wrap a dish towel around your hand to protect it and hold an oyster firmly. Insert an oyster knife or other strong, sharp knife into the hinged edge and twist to prize the shells apart. Still holding both shells firmly in the wrapped hand, slide the blade of the knife along the upper shell to sever the muscle. Lift off the upper shell, being careful not to spill the liquid inside. Slide the blade of the knife along the lower shell underneath the oyster to sever the second muscle. Arrange the oysters on their half-shells in a single layer on a bed of rock salt or crushed ice, if you like.

3 Spoon the dressing evenly over the oysters and serve at room temperature.

Ouster Fritters

SERVES SIX

1/3 cup all-purpose flour
pinch of salt
pinch of sugar
1/4 cup water
2 tsp vegetable oil, plus extra
   for deep-frying
1 egg white
36 fresh oysters, shucked
   (see page 194)
lemon wedges, to garnish

1 Sift the flour, salt, and sugar into a bowl. Stir in the water and vegetable oil until smooth.

2 Heat the oil for deep-frying in a deep-fat fryer or large pan to 350–375°F/180–190°C, or until a cube of bread browns in 30 seconds.

3 Meanwhile, whisk the egg white in a spotlessly clean, greasefree bowl until it forms soft peaks. Gently fold the egg white into the flour mixture until it is fully incorporated.

4 Working in batches, dip the oysters into the batter, then drop them into the hot oil and deep-fry for 3–4 minutes, or until crisp and golden. Remove with a slotted spoon and drain on paper towels. Keep warm while you cook the remaining batches, then serve, garnished with lemon wedges.

Meat & Poultry

MOST MEAT AND POULTRY IS NOT AS PLENTIFUL IN SPAIN AS IT IS IN MANY OTHER COUNTRIES—PORK, INCLUDING CHORIZO SAUSAGE, AND CHICKEN ARE THE MAIN EXCEPTIONS TO THE RULE AND FEATURE HEAVILY IN THIS SECTION. THERE ARE ALSO A COUPLE OF MEATBALL RECIPES—MEATBALLS HAVE BEEN A FEATURE OF SPANISH COOKING SINCE AT LEAST THE THIRTEENTH CENTURY.

MANY OF THESE DISHES WORK EQUALLY WELL WITH ALTERNATIVE MAIN INGREDIENTS: TRY SLICES OF FRESH TURKEY, PORK, OR RABBIT INSTEAD OF THE CHICKEN ON PAGE 223, OR REPLACE THE CHICKEN LIVERS USED ON PAGE 224 WITH LAMB'S OR CALF'S KIDNEYS.

THE DEEP-FRIED STUFFED DATES (SEE PAGE 214) IS ONE REPRESENTATIVE OF THE NEW-STYLE TAPAS RECIPES THAT HAVE DEVELOPED IN MODERN SPANISH METROPOLITAN COCKTAIL BARS.

Miniature Pork Brochettes

MAKES TWELVE

1 lb/450 g lean, boneless pork
3 tbsp Spanish olive oil, plus
    extra for oiling (optional)
grated rind and juice of
    1 large lemon
2 garlic cloves, crushed
2 tbsp chopped fresh
    flatleaf parsley, plus extra
    to garnish
1 tbsp ras-el-hanout spice
    blend
salt and pepper

1 The brochettes are marinated overnight, so remember to do this in advance in order that they are ready when you need them. Cut the pork into pieces about 3/4 inch/2 cm square and put in a large, shallow, nonmetallic dish that will hold the pieces in a single layer.

2 To prepare the marinade, place all the remaining ingredients in a bowl and mix together. Pour the marinade over the pork and toss the meat in it until well coated. Cover the dish and let marinate in the refrigerator for 8 hours or overnight, stirring the pork 2–3 times.

3 You can use wooden or metal skewers to cook the brochettes and for this recipe you will need about 12 x 6-inch/15-cm skewers. If you are using wooden ones, soak them in cold water for 30 minutes prior to using. This helps to stop them burning and the food sticking to them during cooking.

Metal skewers simply need to be greased, and flat ones should be used in preference to round ones to prevent the food on them falling off.

4 Preheat the broiler, grill pan, or grill. Thread 3 marinated pork pieces, leaving a little space between each piece, onto each prepared skewer. Cook the brochettes for 10–15 minutes, or until tender and lightly charred, turning several times and basting with the remaining marinade during cooking. Serve the pork brochettes piping hot, garnished with parsley.

Lamb Skewers with Lemon

SERVES EIGHT

2 garlic cloves, finely
    chopped

1 Spanish onion, finely
    chopped

2 tsp finely grated lemon
    rind

2 tbsp lemon juice

1 tsp fresh thyme leaves

1 tsp ground coriander

1 tsp ground cumin

2 tbsp red wine vinegar

⅓ cup olive oil

2 lb 4 oz/1 kg lamb fillet, cut
    into ¾-inch/2-cm pieces

orange or lemon slices,
    to garnish

1 Mix the garlic, onion, lemon rind, lemon juice, thyme, coriander, cumin, vinegar, and olive oil together in a large, shallow, nonmetallic dish, whisking well until thoroughly combined.

2 Thread the pieces of lamb onto 16 wooden skewers and add to the dish, turning well to coat. Cover with plastic wrap and let marinate in the refrigerator for 2–8 hours, turning occasionally.

3 Preheat the broiler to medium. Drain the skewers, reserving the marinade. Cook under the hot broiler, turning frequently and brushing with the marinade, for 10 minutes, or until tender and cooked to your liking. Serve immediately, garnished with orange slices.

COOK'S TIP: Like quite a few tapas dishes, these little skewers are easy to cook on a grill. Place a couple of large sprigs of fresh rosemary on the hot coals to add extra flavor and aroma.

Tiny Meatballs with Tomato Sauce

MAKES ABOUT SIXTY

olive oil

1 red onion, very finely
chopped

1 lb 2 oz/500 g fresh ground
lamb

1 large egg, beaten

2 tsp freshly squeezed lemon
juice

½ tsp ground cumin

pinch of cayenne pepper,
to taste

2 tbsp very finely chopped
fresh mint

salt and pepper

1¼ cups Tomato & Bell
Pepper Salsa (see page 7),
to serve

1 Heat 1 tablespoon of olive oil in a skillet over medium heat. Add the onion and cook for 5 minutes, stirring occasionally, until softened but not browned.

2 Remove the skillet from the heat and let cool. Add the onion to the lamb with the egg, lemon juice, cumin, cayenne, mint, and salt and pepper to taste in a large bowl. Use your hands to squeeze all the ingredients together. Cook a small piece of the mixture and taste to see if the seasoning needs adjusting.

3 With wet hands, shape the mixture into about 60 x 3/4 -inch/2-cm balls. Place on a tray and let chill for at least 20 minutes.

4 When ready to cook, heat a small amount of olive oil in 1 or 2 large skillets (the exact amount of oil will depend on how much fat is in the lamb). Arrange the meatballs in a single layer, without overcrowding the skillet, and cook over medium heat for 5 minutes, until brown on the outside but still pink inside. Work in batches if necessary, keeping the cooked meatballs warm while you cook the remainder.

5 Gently reheat the Tomato and Bell Pepper Salsa and serve with the meatballs for dipping. These are best served warm with reheated sauce, but they are also enjoyable at room temperature.

Tiny Spanish Meatballs in Almond Sauce

SERVES SIX-EIGHT

2 oz/55 g white or brown
   bread, crusts removed

3 tbsp water

1 lb/450 g fresh ground lean
   pork, beef, or lamb

1 large onion, finely chopped

1 garlic clove, crushed

2 tbsp chopped fresh
   flatleaf parsley, plus extra
   to garnish

1 egg, beaten

freshly grated nutmeg

all-purpose flour, for coating

2 tbsp Spanish olive oil

squeeze of lemon juice,
   to taste

salt and pepper

crusty bread, to serve

ALMOND SAUCE

2 tbsp Spanish olive oil

1 oz/25 g white or brown
   bread

4 oz/115 g blanched almonds

2 garlic cloves, finely
   chopped

2/3 cup dry white wine

generous 1 3/4 cups vegetable
   stock

salt and pepper

1 To prepare the meatballs, place the bread in a bowl, then add the water and let soak for 5 minutes. With your hands, squeeze out the water and return the bread to the dried bowl. Add the pork, onion, garlic, parsley, and egg, then season with grated nutmeg and a little salt and pepper. Knead the ingredients well to form a smooth mixture.

2 Spread some flour on a plate. With floured hands, shape the meat mixture into about 30 equal-size balls, then roll each meatball again in flour until coated.

3 Heat the olive oil in a large, heavy-bottom skillet. Add the meatballs, in batches, and cook for 4–5 minutes, or until browned on all sides. Using a slotted spoon, remove the meatballs from the skillet and reserve.

4 To make the sauce, heat the olive oil in the same skillet in which the meatballs were fried. Break the bread into pieces, then add to the skillet with the almonds and cook gently, stirring frequently, until the bread and almonds are golden brown. Add the garlic and fry for an additional 30 seconds, then pour in the wine and boil for 1–2 minutes. Season

to taste with salt and pepper and let cool slightly.

5 Transfer the almond mixture to a food processor. Pour in the vegetable stock and process the mixture until smooth. Return the sauce to the skillet.

6 Carefully add the meatballs to the almond sauce and simmer for 25 minutes, or until the meatballs are tender. Taste the sauce and season with salt and pepper if necessary.

7 Transfer the cooked meatballs and sauce to a warmed serving dish, then add a squeeze of lemon juice to taste and sprinkle with chopped parsley to garnish. Serve piping hot with crusty bread for mopping up the almond sauce.

Steak Bites with Chili Sauce

SERVES FOUR-SIX

2 tbsp olive oil
1 onion, chopped
1 tsp paprika
1 garlic clove, finely chopped
1 fresh red chili, seeded
   and sliced
14 oz/400 g canned chopped
   tomatoes
2 tbsp dry white wine
1 tbsp tomato paste
1 tbsp sherry vinegar
2 tsp sugar
2 rump steaks, about
   6-8 oz/175-225 g each
2 tsp Tabasco sauce
1 tbsp chopped fresh parsley
salt and pepper

1 Heat half the olive oil in a heavy-bottom saucepan. Add the onion and cook over low heat, stirring occasionally, for 5 minutes, or until softened. Add the paprika, garlic, and chili and cook for an additional 2–3 minutes, then stir in the tomatoes with their juices, wine, tomato paste, vinegar, and sugar. Simmer gently for 15–20 minutes, or until thickened.

2 Meanwhile, heat a heavy-bottom skillet or grill pan over high heat and brush with the remaining olive oil. Season the steaks to taste with pepper and rub with the Tabasco, then add to the pan. Cook for 1–1¹/2 minutes on each side, or until browned. Reduce the heat and cook, turning once, for 3 minutes for rare, 4–5 minutes for medium, or 5–7 minutes for well done. Remove from the heat and keep warm.

3 Transfer the sauce to a food processor or blender and process until fairly smooth. Transfer to a serving bowl, then season to taste with salt and pepper and stir in the parsley.

4 Transfer the steaks to a cutting board and cut into bite-size pieces. Impale on wooden toothpicks, then place on serving plates and serve immediately with the sauce.

Mixed Tapas Platter with Beef

SERVES EIGHT–TEN

7 oz/200 g small waxy
    potatoes, unpeeled
5 tbsp olive oil
2 sirloin steaks, about
    8 oz/225 g each
1 fresh red chili, seeded and
    finely chopped (optional)
12 oz/350 g Queso del
    Montsec or other goat
    cheese, sliced
6 oz/175 g mixed salad greens
2 tbsp black olives
2 tbsp green olives
2 oz/55 g canned anchovies
    in oil, drained and halved
    lengthwise
1 tbsp capers, drained and
    rinsed
salt and pepper

1 Cook the potatoes in a pan of lightly salted boiling water for 15–20 minutes, or until just tender. Drain and let cool slightly.

2 Heat a heavy-bottom skillet or grill pan over high heat and brush with 1 tablespoon of the olive oil. Season the steaks to taste with pepper and add to the pan. Cook for 1–1¹/2 minutes on each side, or until browned. Reduce the heat to medium and cook for 1¹/2 minutes on each side. Remove and rest for 10–15 minutes.

3 Heat 2 tablespoons of the remaining oil in a skillet. Add the chili, if using, and the potatoes and cook, turning frequently, for 10 minutes, or until crisp and golden.

4 Thinly slice the steaks and arrange the slices alternately with the cheese slices along the sides of a serving platter. Mix the salad greens, olives, anchovies, and capers together, then arrange along the center of the platter. Drizzle with the remaining oil, then top with the potatoes. Serve warm or at room temperature.

Beef Skewers with Orange & Garlic

SERVES SIX-EIGHT

3 tbsp white wine

2 tbsp olive oil

3 garlic cloves, finely chopped

juice of 1 orange

1 lb/450 g rump steak, cubed

1 lb/450 g baby onions, halved

2 orange bell peppers, seeded and cut into squares

8 oz/225 g cherry tomatoes, halved

salt and pepper

1 Mix the wine, olive oil, garlic, and orange juice together in a shallow, nonmetallic dish. Add the cubes of steak, season to taste with salt and pepper, and toss to coat. Cover with plastic wrap and let marinate in the refrigerator for 2–8 hours.

3 Cook the skewers under the hot broiler, turning and brushing frequently with the marinade, for 10 minutes, or until cooked through. Transfer to warmed serving plates and serve immediately.

2 Preheat the broiler to high. Drain the steak, reserving the marinade. Thread the steak, onions, bell peppers, and tomatoes alternately onto several small skewers.

Serrano Ham with Arugula

SERVES SIX

5 oz/140 g arugula, separated into leaves

4½ tbsp olive oil

1½ tbsp orange juice

10 oz/280 g thinly sliced serrano ham

salt and pepper

COOK'S TIP: Jamón de Jabugo from the Huelva region is the ideal ham for this tapa, as its intrinsic sweetness contrasts beautifully with the peppery flavor of arugula.

1 Place the arugula in a bowl and pour in the olive oil and orange juice. Season to taste with salt and pepper and toss well.

2 Arrange the slices of ham on individual serving plates, folding it into attractive shapes. Divide the arugula between the plates and serve immediately.

Cheese & Ham Pastries

SERVES SIX

6 slices serrano ham
Tabasco sauce, for brushing
7 oz/200 g Queso Majorero,
  Manchego, or goat cheese
6 sheets phyllo pastry, about
  18 x 11 inches/46 x 28 cm
3-4 tbsp olive oil

COOK'S TIP: Phyllo is not, of course, a typically Spanish ingredient, although ouarka, a similar pastry from North Africa, is found in southern Spain.

1 Preheat the oven to 400°F/200°C. Spread out the ham and brush with Tabasco to taste. Cut the cheese into 6 slices. Wrap a slice of cheese in each slice of ham.

2 Working on one sheet of pastry at a time and keeping the others covered with a clean, damp tea towel, brush with a little olive oil, then fold in half. Place 1 ham-wrapped slice of cheese in the center, then brush the pastry with oil again and fold it over to enclose it completely. Place on a baking sheet, seam-side down, and brush the top with a little oil. Repeat with the remaining sheets of phyllo and ham-wrapped cheese.

3 Bake in the preheated oven for 15 minutes, or until golden brown and crisp. Serve immediately or let cool slightly and serve warm.

Ham & Almond Fritters

SERVES FOUR-SIX

1/2 cup all-purpose flour
2/3 cup water
1/2 stick butter
2 eggs
2 oz/55 g slivered almonds
4 oz/115 g ham, chopped
vegetable oil, for deep-frying
salt and pepper

1 Sift the flour with a pinch of salt and pepper onto a sheet of waxed paper. Bring the water to a boil in a heavy-bottom pan. Add the butter and as soon as it has melted, remove the pan from the heat. Tip in the flour and beat well with a wooden spoon until the mixture comes away from the side of the pan.

2 Beat in the eggs, one at a time, and continue to beat until the mixture is glossy. Fold in the slivered almonds and ham and let the mixture cool.

3 Heat the vegetable oil in a deep-fat fryer or large pan to

350–375°F/180–190°C, or until a cube of bread browns in 30 seconds.

4 Working in batches, drop heaped tablespoonfuls of the mixture into the hot oil and deep-fry for 3–4 minutes, or until crisp and golden. Remove with a slotted spoon and drain on paper towels. Serve the fritters hot.

Chorizo & Mushroom Kabobs

MAKES TWENTY-FIVE

2 tbsp olive oil

25 pieces chorizo sausage,
each about
½-inch/1-cm square
(about 3½ oz/100 g)

25 white mushrooms, wiped
and stems removed

1 green bell pepper, broiled,
peeled, and cut into
5 squares

1 Heat the olive oil in a skillet over medium heat. Add the chorizo and cook for 20 seconds, stirring.

2 Add the mushrooms and continue cooking for an additional 1–2 minutes until the mushrooms begin to brown and absorb the fat in the skillet.

3 Thread a bell pepper square, a piece of chorizo, and a mushroom onto a wooden toothpick. Continue until all the ingredients are used. Serve hot or at room temperature.

Deep-Fried Stuffed Dates

SERVES SIX

1 ready-to-eat chorizo
    sausage
12 fresh dates
6 bacon strips, rinds removed
2 tbsp all-purpose flour,
    for dusting
1 egg, lightly beaten
1 cup fresh white bread
    crumbs
vegetable oil, for deep-frying

1 Remove the outer casing from the chorizo and cut the sausage into 3 slices. Cut each slice into fourths.

2 Slit the sides of the dates with a sharp knife and remove and discard the pits. Insert a piece of chorizo into each cavity. Stretch the bacon strips with the back of a knife, then cut each strip in half across the center. Wrap a piece of bacon around each date.

3 Place the flour, egg, and bread crumbs in separate shallow dishes. Coat the dates in the flour, then in the egg, then in the bread crumbs. Meanwhile, heat the vegetable oil in a deep-fat fryer or large pan to 350–375°F/180–190°C, or until a cube of bread browns in 30 seconds.

4 Deep-fry the stuffed dates, in batches if necessary, turning them occasionally, for 3–4 minutes, or until golden brown all over. Remove with a slotted spoon and drain on paper towels. Serve hot.

Chorizo Empanadillas

MAKES TWELVE

4½ oz/125 g chorizo sausage,
    outer casing removed
9 oz/250 g ready-made puff
    pastry, thawed if frozen
all-purpose flour, for dusting
beaten egg, to glaze

TO GARNISH

paprika
fresh basil sprigs

1 Preheat the oven to 400°F/200°C. Cut the chorizo into small dice measuring about 1/2 inch/1 cm square. Thinly roll out the puff pastry on a lightly floured counter. Using a plain, round 3 1/4-inch/8-cm cutter, cut into rounds. Gently pile the trimmings together and roll out again, then cut out additional circles to produce 12 in total.

2 Place about 1 teaspoon of the chopped chorizo onto each of the pastry rounds. Dampen the edges of the pastry with a little water, then fold one half over the other half to completely cover the chorizo. Seal the edges together with your fingers. Using the tines

of a fork, press against the edges to give a decorative finish and seal them further. With the point of a sharp knife, make a small slit in the side of each pastry. You can store the pastries in the refrigerator at this stage until you are ready to bake them.

3 Place the pastries onto dampened baking sheets and

brush each with a little beaten egg to glaze. Bake in the preheated oven for 10–15 minutes, or until golden brown and puffed. Using a small strainer, lightly dust the top of each empanadilla with a little paprika and garnish with herb sprigs. Serve hot or warm.

Chorizo & Quails' Eggs

MAKES TWELVE

12 slices French bread, sliced on the diagonal, about 1/4 inch/5 mm thick

1½ oz/40 g cured, ready-to-eat chorizo, cut into 12 thin slices

olive oil

12 quails' eggs

mild paprika

salt and pepper

fresh flatleaf parsley, to garnish

1 Preheat the broiler to high. Arrange the slices of bread on a baking sheet and broil until golden brown on both sides.

2 Cut or fold the chorizo slices to fit on the toasts, then reserve.

3 Heat a thin layer of olive oil in a large skillet over medium heat until a cube of bread sizzles—about 40 seconds. Break the eggs into the skillet and cook, spooning the fat over the yolks, until the whites are set and the yolks are cooked to your liking.

4 Remove the fried eggs from the skillet and drain on paper towels. Immediately transfer to the chorizo-topped toasts and dust with paprika. Season to taste with salt and pepper, then garnish with parsley and serve immediately.

Chorizo in Red Wine

SERVES SIX

7 oz/200 g chorizo sausage
generous 3/4 cup Spanish red
  wine
2 tbsp brandy (optional)
fresh flatleaf parsley sprigs,
  to garnish
crusty bread, to serve

1 Before you begin, bear in mind that this dish is best if prepared the day before you are planning to serve it. Using a fork, prick the chorizo in 3 or 4 places and pour wine over. Place the chorizo and wine in a large pan. Bring the wine to a boil, then reduce the heat and simmer gently, covered, for 15–20 minutes. Transfer the chorizo and wine to a bowl or dish, cover and let the sausage marinate in the wine for 8 hours or overnight.

2 The next day, remove the chorizo from the bowl or dish and reserve the wine. Remove the outer casing from the chorizo and cut the sausage into $^1/_4$-inch/5-mm slices. Place the slices in a large, heavy-bottom skillet or flameproof serving dish.

3 If you are adding the brandy, pour it into a small pan and heat gently. Pour the brandy over the chorizo slices, then stand well back and set alight. When the flames have died down, shake the pan gently and add the reserved wine to the pan, then cook over high heat until almost all of the wine has evaporated.

4 Serve the chorizo in red wine piping hot, in the dish in which it was cooked, sprinkled with parsley to garnish. Accompany with chunks or slices of bread to mop up the juices and provide wooden toothpicks to spear the pieces of chorizo.

Fried Chorizo with Herbs

SERVES SIX-EIGHT

1 lb 9 oz/700 g chorizo
   cooking sausage
2 tbsp olive oil
2 garlic cloves, finely
   chopped
4 tbsp chopped mixed fresh
   herbs

1 Using a sharp knife, cut the chorizo into $^1/4$-inch/5-mm thick slices. Heat a large, heavy-bottom skillet. Add the chorizo slices, without any additional fat, and cook over medium heat, stirring frequently, for 5 minutes, or until crisp and browned.

3 Heat the olive oil in the skillet over a medium–low heat. Add the chorizo slices, garlic, and herbs and cook, stirring occasionally, until heated through. Serve immediately.

2 Remove the chorizo slices with a spatula or slotted spoon and drain well on paper towels. Drain the fat from the skillet and wipe out with a pad of paper towels.

COOK'S TIP: Chorizo may be mild or hot and it is available both smoked and unsmoked. All types of cooking sausage are suitable for this dish.

Chickpeas & Chorizo

SERVES FOUR-SIX

9 oz/250 g chorizo sausage
   in 1 piece, outer casing
   removed
4 tbsp olive oil
1 onion, finely chopped
1 large garlic clove, crushed
14 oz/400 g canned
   chickpeas, drained and
   rinsed
6 pimientos del piquillo
   (see page 160), drained,
   patted dry and sliced
1 tbsp sherry vinegar,
   or to taste
salt and pepper
finely chopped fresh parsley
   to garnish
crusty bread slices, to serve

1 Cut the chorizo into 1/2-inch/1-cm dice. Heat the oil in a heavy-bottom skillet over medium heat, then add the onion and garlic. Cook, stirring occasionally, until the onion is softened but not browned. Stir in the chorizo and cook until heated through.

2 Tip the mixture into a bowl and stir in the chickpeas and pimientos. Splash with sherry vinegar and season to taste with salt and pepper. Serve hot or at room temperature, generously sprinkled with parsley, with plenty of crusty bread.

Chicken in Lemon & Garlic

SERVES SIX–EIGHT

4 large skinless, boneless
   chicken breasts
5 tbsp Spanish olive oil
1 onion, finely chopped
6 garlic cloves, finely chopped
grated rind of 1 lemon, finely
   pared rind of 1 lemon, and
   juice of both lemons
4 tbsp chopped fresh
   flatleaf parsley, plus extra
   to garnish
salt and pepper

TO SERVE

lemon wedges
crusty bread

1 Using a sharp knife, slice the chicken breasts widthwise into thin slices. Heat the oil in a heavy-bottom skillet. Add the onion and cook for 5 minutes, or until softened but not browned. Add the garlic and cook for an additional 30 seconds.

2 Add the sliced chicken to the skillet and cook gently for 5–10 minutes, stirring occasionally, until all the ingredients are lightly browned and the chicken is tender.

3 Add the grated lemon rind and the lemon juice and let it bubble. At the same time, deglaze the skillet by scraping and stirring

all the bits on the bottom of the skillet into the juices with a wooden spoon. Remove the skillet from the heat, then stir in the parsley and season to taste with salt and pepper.

4 Transfer the chicken in lemon and garlic, piping hot, to a warmed serving dish. Sprinkle with the pared lemon rind and

garnish with parsley sprigs. Serve with lemon wedges for squeezing over the chicken, accompanied by chunks or slices of crusty bread for mopping up the lemon and garlic juices.

Chicken Livers in Sherry Sauce

SERVES SIX

1 lb/450 g chicken livers

2 tbsp Spanish olive oil

1 small onion, finely chopped

2 garlic cloves, finely
   chopped

scant ½ cup dry Spanish
   sherry

2 tbsp chopped fresh
   flatleaf parsley, plus extra
   sprigs, to garnish

salt and pepper

crusty bread or toast,
   to serve

1 If necessary, trim the livers, cutting away any ducts and gristle, then cut into small, bite-size pieces. Heat the oil in a large, heavy-bottom skillet. Add the onion and cook for 5 minutes, or until softened but not browned. Add the garlic and cook for an additional 30 seconds.

2 Add the livers to the skillet and cook for 2–3 minutes, stirring constantly, until they are firm and have changed color on the outside but are still pink and soft in the center. Using a slotted spoon, lift the livers from the skillet and transfer to a large, warmed serving dish or several smaller ones. Keep warm.

3 Add the sherry to the skillet, increase the heat, and let it bubble for 3–4 minutes to evaporate the alcohol and reduce slightly. At the same time, deglaze the skillet by scraping and stirring all the bits on the base of the skillet into the sauce with a wooden spoon. Season the sauce to taste with salt and pepper.

4 Pour the sherry sauce over the chicken livers and sprinkle over the parsley. Garnish with parsley sprigs and serve piping hot with chunks or slices of crusty bread or toast to mop up the sauce.

Spicy Chicken Livers

SERVES FOUR-SIX

generous ¾ cup all-purpose
  flour
½ tsp ground cumin
½ tsp ground coriander
½ tsp paprika
¼ tsp freshly grated nutmeg
12 oz/350 g chicken livers
6 tbsp olive oil
salt and pepper
fresh mint sprigs, to garnish

1 Sift the flour onto a large, shallow plate and stir in the cumin, coriander, paprika, and nutmeg. Season to taste with salt and pepper.

2 Trim the chicken livers and pat dry with paper towels. Cut the livers in halves or fourths. Toss in the seasoned flour, a few pieces at a time, shaking off any excess.

3 Heat the olive oil in a large, heavy-bottom skillet. Cook the livers, in batches, over high heat, stirring frequently, for 3–5 minutes, or until crisp on the outside but still tender in the center. Serve impaled on wooden toothpicks and garnished with mint sprigs.

Chicken Wings with Tomato Dressing

SERVES SIX-EIGHT

¾ cup olive oil

3 garlic cloves, finely chopped

1 tsp ground cumin

2 lb 4 oz/1 kg chicken wings

2 tomatoes, peeled, seeded (see page 167), and diced

5 tbsp white wine vinegar

1 tbsp shredded fresh basil leaves

1 Preheat the oven to 350°F/180°C. Mix 1 tablespoon of the oil, the garlic, and cumin together in a shallow dish. Cut off and discard the tips of the chicken wings and add the wings to the spice mixture, turning to coat. Cover with plastic wrap and let marinate in a cool place for 15 minutes.

2 Heat 3 tablespoons of the remaining oil in a large, heavy-bottom skillet. Add the chicken wings, in batches, and cook, turning frequently, until golden brown. Transfer to a roasting pan.

3 Roast the chicken wings for 10–15 minutes, or until tender and the juices run clear when the point of a sharp knife is inserted into the thickest part of the meat.

4 Meanwhile, mix the remaining olive oil, the tomatoes, vinegar and basil together in a bowl.

5 Using tongs, transfer the chicken wings to a nonmetallic dish. Pour the dressing over them, turning to coat. Cover with plastic wrap and let cool, then chill for 4 hours. Remove from the refrigerator 30–60 minutes before serving to return to room temperature.

Chicken Rolls with Olives

SERVES SIX-EIGHT
²/₃ cup black olives in oil,
    drained
1¼ sticks butter, softened
4 tbsp chopped fresh parsley
4 skinless, boneless
    chicken breasts
2 tbsp oil from the olive jar

1 Preheat the oven to 400°F/200°C. Pit and chop the olives. Mix half the olives, the butter, and parsley together in a bowl.

2 Place the chicken breasts between 2 sheets of plastic wrap and beat gently with a meat mallet or the side of a rolling pin.

3 Spread the olive and herb butter over one side of each flattened chicken breast and roll up. Secure with a wooden toothpick or tie with clean string if necessary.

4 Place the chicken rolls in an ovenproof dish. Drizzle over

the oil from the olive jar and bake in the preheated oven for 45–55 minutes, or until tender and the juices run clear when the chicken is pierced with the point of a sharp knife.

5 Transfer the chicken rolls to a cutting board and discard the cocktail sticks or string. Using a sharp knife, cut into slices, then transfer to warmed serving plates and serve.

Crispy Chicken & Ham Croquettes

MAKES EIGHT

4 tbsp olive oil or ½ stick butter

4 tbsp all-purpose flour

generous ¾ cup milk

4 oz/115 g cooked chicken, ground

2 oz/55 g serrano or cooked ham, very finely chopped

1 tbsp chopped fresh flatleaf parsley, plus extra sprigs to garnish

small pinch of freshly grated nutmeg

1 egg, beaten

1 cup day-old white bread crumbs

corn oil, for deep-frying

salt and pepper

Aïoli (see page 12), to serve

1 Heat the olive oil or butter in a pan. Stir in the flour to form a paste and cook gently for 1 minute, stirring constantly. Remove the pan from the heat and gradually stir in the milk until smooth. Return to the heat and slowly bring to a boil, stirring constantly, until the mixture thickens.

2 Remove the pan from the heat, add the ground chicken and beat until the mixture is smooth. Add the chopped ham, parsley, and nutmeg and mix well. Season the mixture to taste with salt and pepper. Spread the chicken mixture in a dish and let stand for 30 minutes until cool, then cover and let chill for 2–3 hours or overnight. Don't be tempted to miss out this stage, as chilling the croquettes helps to stop them falling apart when they are cooked.

3 When the chicken mixture has chilled, pour the beaten egg onto a plate and spread the bread crumbs out on a separate plate. Divide the chicken mixture into 8 equal-size portions. With dampened hands, form each portion into a cylindrical shape. Dip the croquettes, one at a time, in the beaten egg, then roll in the bread crumbs to coat them. Place on a plate and let chill for 1 hour.

4 To cook, heat the corn oil in a deep-fat fryer to 350–375°F/ 180–190°C, or until a cube of bread browns in 30 seconds. Add the croquettes, in batches to prevent the temperature of the oil dropping, and deep-fry for 5–10 minutes, or until golden brown and crispy. Remove with a slotted spoon and drain well on paper towels.

5 Serve the chicken and ham croquettes piping hot, garnished with parsley sprigs and accompanied by a bowl of Aïoli for dipping.

Bread & Pizzas

CONSIDERING THE EVOLUTION OF TAPAS FROM THE ORIGINAL SLICES OF BREAD, TOPPED WITH SIMPLE INGREDIENTS, TO A COSMOPOLITAN AND VARIED CUISINE ENJOYED THE WORLD OVER, IT SEEMS FITTING TO END THIS BOOK WITH A SELECTION OF BREAD-BASED RECIPES AND DISHES THAT SHARE A LINEAGE WITH THE COOKING OF OTHER NATIONS. THE SHRIMP TOASTIES (SEE PAGE 248) ARE ACTUALLY A LOCAL PIZZA-STYLE DISH. VARIATIONS INCLUDE MANY TOPPINGS FOUND ON PIZZAS, SUCH AS ANCHOVIES, PEPPERS, AND HAM, BUT SELDOM CHEESE. THE CHORIZO PIZZA (SEE PAGE 252) IS, HOWEVER, AN ITALIAN-STYLE PIZZA WITH A SPANISH TWIST.

Flat Bread with Vegetables & Clams

SERVES FOUR-SIX

2 tbsp extra-virgin olive oil

4 large garlic cloves, crushed

2 large onions, thinly sliced

10 pimientos del piquillo (see page 160), drained, patted dry, and thinly sliced

9 oz/250 g shelled baby clams in brine (weight in jar), drained and rinsed

salt and pepper

DOUGH

2⅔ cups white bread flour, plus extra for dusting

1 envelope active dry yeast

1 tsp salt

½ tsp sugar

1 tbsp olive oil, plus extra for oiling

1 tbsp dry white wine

1 cup warm water

1 To make the dough, stir the flour, yeast, salt, and sugar together in a bowl, making a well in the center. Add the olive oil and wine to the water, then pour 1/4 cup of the liquid into the well. Gradually mix in the flour from the sides, adding the remaining liquid if necessary, until a soft dough forms.

2 Turn out the dough onto a lightly floured counter and knead until smooth. Shape the dough into a ball. Wash the bowl and rub the inside with olive oil. Return the dough to the bowl and roll it around until lightly coated in oil. Cover the bowl tightly with plastic wrap and let stand in a warm place until the dough doubles in size.

3 Heat the olive oil in a large, heavy-bottom skillet over medium heat. Reduce the heat and add the garlic and onions and cook slowly, stirring frequently, for 25 minutes, or until the onions are golden brown but not burned.

4 Preheat the oven to 450°F/230°C. Transfer the onions to a bowl and let cool. Add the sweet pepper strips and clams to the bowl and stir together. Reserve.

5 Knock back the dough and knead quickly on a lightly floured counter. Cover it with the upturned bowl and let stand for 10 minutes, which will make it easier to roll out.

6 Heavily flour a 12 3/4 x 12 3/4-inch/32 x 32-cm shallow baking sheet. Roll out the dough to make a 13 1/2-inch/34-cm square and transfer it to the baking sheet, rolling the edges to form a thin rim. Prick the base all over with a fork.

7 Spread the topping evenly over the dough and season to taste with salt and pepper. Bake in the preheated oven for 25 minutes, or until the rim is golden brown and the onion tips are slightly tinged. Transfer to a wire rack to cool completely. Cut into 12–16 slices.

Salads on Bread

EACH SALAD QUANTITY
MAKES 12-14 OPEN
SANDWICHES
POTATO SALAD

7 oz/200 g new potatoes,
   scrubbed and boiled
½ tbsp white wine vinegar
3-4 tbsp mayonnaise
2 hard-cooked eggs, shelled
   and finely chopped
2 scallions, white and green
   parts finely chopped
1 large French bread
salt and pepper
12-14 black olives, pitted and
   sliced, to garnish

TUNA SALAD

7 oz/200 g canned tuna in
   olive oil, drained
4 tbsp mayonnaise
2 hard-cooked eggs, shelled
   and finely chopped
1 tomato, broiled and peeled,
   seeded (see page 167),
   and very finely chopped
2 tsp grated lemon rind, or
   to taste
cayenne pepper, to taste
1 large French bread
salt and pepper
12-14 anchovy fillets in oil,
   drained, to garnish

1 To make the potato salad, peel the potatoes as soon as they are cool enough to handle, then cut into $^1/_4$ -inch/5-mm dice. Toss with the vinegar and season to taste with salt and pepper. Let cool completely. Stir in the mayonnaise, then fold in the eggs and scallions. Taste and adjust the seasoning. Cut the bread on a slight diagonal into 24–28 slices, $^1/_4$ inch/5 mm thick. Mound the salad on the bread, then top with olive slices.

2 To make the tuna salad, flake the tuna into a bowl. Stir in the mayonnaise, then fold in the eggs, tomato, lemon rind, and cayenne. Taste and adjust the seasoning. Cut the bread on a slight diagonal into 24–28 slices, $^1/_4$ inch/5 mm thick. Mound the salad on the bread, then top with anchovy fillets.

Spicy Fried Bread & Chorizo

SERVES SIX-EIGHT

7 oz/200 g chorizo sausage, outer casing removed

4 thick slices 2-day-old country bread

Spanish olive oil, for shallow-frying

3 garlic cloves, finely chopped

2 tbsp chopped fresh flatleaf parsley

paprika, to garnish

1 Cut the chorizo into 1/2 -inch/1-cm thick slices and cut the bread, with its crusts still on, into 1/2 -inch/1-cm cubes. Add enough olive oil to a large, heavy-bottom skillet so that it generously covers the base. Heat the oil, then add the garlic and cook for 30 seconds–1 minute, or until lightly browned.

2 Add the bread cubes to the pan and cook, stirring constantly, until golden brown and crisp. Add the chorizo slices and cook for 1–2 minutes, or until hot. Using a slotted spoon, remove the bread cubes and chorizo from the skillet and drain well on paper towels.

3 Turn the bread and chorizo into a warmed serving bowl, then add the chopped parsley and toss together. Garnish the dish with a sprinkling of paprika and serve warm. Accompany with wooden toothpicks so that a piece of sausage and a cube of bread can be speared together for eating.

Crusty Bread with Beans & Chorizo

SERVES SIX

3 garlic cloves

4 tbsp olive oil

1 Spanish onion, finely
  chopped

5 oz/140 g chorizo cooking
  sausage, sliced

1 lb 12 oz/800 g canned
  haricot beans, drained
  and rinsed

6 thick slices country bread

4 tomatoes, chopped

salt and pepper

fresh parsley sprigs,
  to garnish

1 Thinly slice 2 of the garlic cloves. Heat half the olive oil in a heavy-bottom skillet. Add the onion and sliced garlic and cook over low heat, stirring occasionally, for 5 minutes, or until softened. Meanwhile, cut the chorizo slices in half.

2 Stir the chorizo into the skillet and cook for an additional 2 minutes, then add the beans. Season to taste with salt and pepper.

3 Grill or toast the bread on both sides. Meanwhile, stir the tomatoes into the skillet.

4 Halve the remaining garlic clove and rub the cut sides over the toast, then drizzle the toast with the remaining oil.

5 Place the grilled bread on individual serving plates and divide the bean and chorizo mixture between the slices. Serve immediately, garnished with parsley sprigs.

Little Breads with Bean Purée

SERVES FOUR

1 ⅓ cups dried great
   Northern beans
½ onion, finely chopped
2 tbsp olive oil
2 tbsp chopped fresh mint
4 thick slices country bread
salt and pepper

COOK'S TIP: Cover the bowl
of bean purée with plastic wrap
and store in the refrigerator
until required. Return to room
temperature before serving.

1 Place the beans in a bowl and add enough cold water to cover. Let soak for 4 hours, or preferably overnight, then drain.

2 Place the beans in a pan and add the onion. Pour in just enough water to cover the beans and onion and bring to a boil. Cook for 1 ½ hours, or until tender, then drain well and let cool slightly.

3 Toast the bread on both sides. Transfer the beans to a food processor or blender and process to a purée. Scrape into a serving bowl and stir in the olive oil and mint. Season to taste with salt and pepper. Divide the purée between the slices of bread and serve at room temperature.

Salt Cod on Garlic Toasts

SERVES SIX

7 oz/200 g dried salt cod
5 garlic cloves
1 cup olive oil
1 cup heavy cream
6 thick slices country bread
pepper

tender. Drain well and let stand until cool enough to handle.

2 Finely chop 4 of the garlic cloves. Halve the remaining clove and reserve until required.

3 Remove and discard the skin from the fish. Coarsely chop the flesh and place in a food processor or blender.

4 Pour the olive oil into a pan and add the chopped garlic. Bring to simmering point over low heat. Pour the cream into a separate pan and bring to simmering point over low heat. Remove both pans from the heat.

1 Soak the dried salt cod in cold water for 48 hours, changing the water 3 times a day. Drain well, then cut into chunks and place in a large, shallow skillet. Pour in enough cold water to cover and bring to simmering point. Poach for 8–10 minutes, or until

5 Process the fish briefly. With the motor still running, add a little of the garlic oil and process. With the motor still running, add a little cream and process. Continue in this way until all the garlic oil and cream have been incorporated. Scrape the mixture into a serving bowl and season to taste with pepper.

6 Toast the bread on both sides, then rub each slice with the cut sides of the reserved garlic. Pile the fish mixture onto the toasts and serve.

Tomato Bread

SERVES FOUR

sliced bread or French
   bread
tomatoes
garlic (optional)
olive oil (optional)

VARIATION: For a more
substantial snack, serve tomato
bread with a plate of thinly
sliced serrano ham and
Manchego cheese, and let
guests assemble open sandwiches

1 At its simplest, slices of bread
are simply rubbed with half a
fresh juicy tomato. If the bread is
soft, you can toast it first. Other
options are to flavor it with garlic,
or drizzle olive oil over the top.

Tomato Toasts with Three Toppings

SERVES FOUR-SIX

12 thick slices country bread

12 tomatoes, peeled, seeded (see page 167), and diced

8 garlic cloves, finely chopped

about 1½ cups olive oil

salt and pepper

HAM & CAPER TOPPING

2 slices ham, cut into thin strips

8 capers, drained and rinsed

CHORIZO & CHEESE TOPPING

8 slices ready-to-eat chorizo sausage

2 oz/55 g Manchego or Cheddar cheese, sliced

2 pimiento-stuffed olives, halved

ANCHOVY & OLIVE TOPPING

12 canned anchovy fillets in oil, drained

4 anchovy-stuffed green olives

1 Toast the bread on both sides. Meanwhile, place the tomatoes in a bowl and break up with a fork, then mix in the garlic. Spread the tomato mixture evenly over the toast, then season to taste with salt and pepper and drizzle with the olive oil.

2 For the ham and caper topping, arrange the strips of ham in an "S" shape across 4 of the toasts. Place a caper in the curves of each letter "S."

3 For the chorizo and cheese topping, place 2 slices of chorizo on each of 4 of the remaining toasts and top with the cheese. Garnish with an olive half.

4 For the anchovy and olive topping, curl 3 anchovy fillets into circles. Place on the remaining 4 toasts and put an olive in the center of each.

Broiled Tomatoes on Bread

SERVES FOUR

3 tbsp olive oil

6 tomatoes, thickly sliced

4 thick slices country bread

1 garlic clove, halved

4 tsp sherry vinegar

salt and pepper

VARIATION: For a garnish, add a few shavings of Manchego, Queso Iberico, or other hard cheese.

1 Heat a ridged griddle pan and brush with 1 tablespoon of the olive oil. Add the tomato slices and cook over high heat for 2 minutes on each side, or until softened and beginning to char.

2 Meanwhile, toast the bread on both sides, then rub each slice with the cut sides of the garlic.

3 Divide the tomato slices between the slices of toast and drizzle with the remaining oil and the vinegar. Season to taste with salt and pepper and serve.

Asparagus Rolls

SERVES EIGHT

1 stick butter, softened, plus
  extra for greasing
8 asparagus spears, trimmed
8 slices white bread, crusts
  removed
1 tbsp chopped fresh parsley
finely grated rind of 1 orange
salt and pepper

1 Preheat the oven to 375°F/190°C and lightly grease a baking sheet. If woody, peel the asparagus stems, then tie the spears loosely together with clean kitchen string. Blanch in a tall pan of boiling water for 3–5 minutes. Drain and refresh under cold running water. Drain again and pat dry with paper towels.

2 Lightly flatten the slices of bread with a rolling pin. Mix generous 1/2 stick of the butter, the parsley, and orange rind together in a bowl and season to taste with salt and pepper. Spread the flavored butter over the bread slices.

3 Place an asparagus spear near one side of a bread slice and roll up. Repeat with the remaining asparagus spears and bread. Place the asparagus rolls, seam-side down, on the baking sheet.

4 Melt the remaining butter in a small pan, then brush it over the asparagus rolls. Bake in the preheated oven for 15 minutes, or until crisp and golden brown. Let cool slightly, then serve warm.

Anchovy Rolls

SERVES FOUR

butter, for greasing and
    spreading
8 salted anchovies
¼ cup milk
4 slices white bread, crusts
    removed
1 tbsp Dijon mustard
2 tbsp grated Manchego or
    Cheddar cheese

1 Preheat the oven to 425°F/220°C. Lightly grease a baking sheet. Place the anchovies in a small, shallow dish and pour over the milk. Let soak for 10–15 minutes. Drain, discarding the milk, and pat dry with paper towels.

2 Spread each bread slice with butter and then with mustard. Sprinkle with the grated cheese. Divide the anchovy between the bread slices and roll up.

3 Place on the baking sheet, seam-side down, and bake in the preheated oven for 6–7 minutes. Let cool slightly, then serve.

Olive & Red Bell Pepper Bread

SERVES FOUR-SIX

2 red bell peppers, halved
  and seeded
3 garlic cloves
2 tsp capers, drained, rinsed,
  and halved
4 tbsp chopped fresh parsley
1 tbsp lemon juice
1 tsp ground cumin
2 tsp sugar
1/3 cup black olives, pitted
  and chopped
1 French bread
2 tbsp olive oil

1 Preheat the broiler to high. Place the bell pepper halves, skin-side up, in a single layer on a baking sheet. Cook under the hot broiler for 8–10 minutes, or until the skin is blackened and blistered all over. Using tongs, transfer to a plastic bag, then tie the top and let cool. When cool enough to handle, peel off the skin.

2 Finely chop 1 of the garlic cloves. Place in a food processor or blender with the bell pepper halves, capers, parsley, lemon juice, cumin, and sugar and process until smooth. Scrape the mixture into a bowl and stir in the olives.

3 Cut off and discard the crusty ends of the bread, then cut the bread into ¹/2-inch/1-cm slices. Toast the slices on both sides. Cut the remaining garlic cloves in half, then rub the cut sides all over the toast. Brush the toast with the olive oil.

4 Spoon the bell pepper mixture onto the toasted bread and place on a serving platter. Serve immediately.

Onion & Olive Circles

SERVES FOUR-EIGHT

2 tbsp olive oil

1 onion, thinly sliced

1 garlic clove, finely chopped

2 tsp chopped fresh thyme

1 small French bread

1 tbsp tapenade or butter

8 canned anchovy fillets in
    oil, drained

12 olives stuffed with
    almonds or onion, halved

salt and pepper

1 Heat the olive oil in a heavy-bottom skillet. Add the onion and garlic and cook over low heat, stirring occasionally, for 15 minutes, or until golden brown and very soft. Stir in the thyme and season to taste with salt and pepper.

2 Meanwhile, cut off and discard the crusty ends of the bread, then cut the loaf into 8 slices. Toast on both sides, then spread with tapenade or butter.

3 Pile the onion mixture onto the slices of toast and top each slice with an anchovy fillet and the olives. Serve hot.

Shrimp Toasties

SERVES FOUR

3 garlic cloves

4 tbsp olive oil

1 Spanish onion, halved and finely chopped

14 oz/400 g canned great Northern beans, drained and rinsed

4 tomatoes, diced

4 thick slices country bread

10 oz/280 g cooked shelled shrimp

salt and pepper

watercress, to garnish

1 Halve 1 of the garlic cloves and reserve. Finely chop the remaining cloves. Heat 2 tablespoons of the olive oil in a large, heavy-bottom skillet. Add the chopped garlic and onion and cook over low heat, stirring occasionally, for 5 minutes, or until softened.

2 Stir in the beans and tomatoes and season to taste with salt and pepper. Cook gently for an additional 5 minutes.

3 Meanwhile, toast the bread on both sides, then rub each slice with the cut sides of the reserved garlic and drizzle with the remaining oil.

4 Stir the shrimp into the bean mixture and heat through gently for 2–3 minutes. Pile the bean and shrimp mixture onto the toasts and serve immediately, garnished with watercress.

Eggplant & Goat Cheese Toasties

SERVES FOUR

5 tbsp olive oil
2 eggplants, sliced
2 tomatoes, halved
2 tsp chopped fresh thyme
4 oz/115 g goat cheese, crumbled
4 thick slices country bread
1 garlic clove, halved
salt and pepper

1 Heat a grill pan and brush with 1 tablespoon of the olive oil. Add the eggplant slices and tomato halves and cook over medium heat, turning occasionally, for 5 minutes. Transfer to a cutting board and coarsely chop.

2 Transfer the eggplants to a bowl and stir in the thyme and about half the cheese. Drizzle with 2–3 tablespoons of the remaining olive oil and season to taste with salt and pepper, mixing well. Meanwhile, preheat the broiler to medium.

3 Toast the bread under the hot broiler on both sides. Rub each slice with the cut sides of the garlic and drizzle with the remaining oil.

4 Pile the eggplant mixture onto the toasts, spreading it out, and sprinkle with the remaining cheese. Cook under the hot broiler for 2–3 minutes, or until hot and bubbling. Serve immediately.

Spanish Spinach & Tomato Pizzas

MAKES THIRTY-TWO

2 tbsp Spanish olive oil, plus extra for brushing and drizzling
1 onion, finely chopped
1 garlic clove, finely chopped
14 oz/400 g canned chopped tomatoes
4½ oz/125 g fresh baby spinach
2 tbsp pine nuts
salt and pepper

BREAD DOUGH

scant ⅓ cup warm water
½ tsp active dry yeast
pinch of sugar
1⅓ cups white bread flour, plus extra for dusting
½ tsp salt

1 To make the bread dough, measure the water into a small bowl. Sprinkle in the dried yeast and sugar and let stand in a warm place for 10–15 minutes, or until frothy.

2 Meanwhile, sift the flour and salt into a large bowl. Make a well in the center and pour in the yeast liquid, then mix together with a spoon. Using your hands, work the mixture until it leaves the sides of the bowl clean.

3 Turn the dough out onto a lightly floured counter and knead for 10 minutes, or until smooth and elastic and no longer sticky. Shape into a ball and put it in a clean bowl. Cover with a clean, damp tea towel and let stand in a warm place for 1 hour, or until it has risen.

4 To make the topping, heat the olive oil in a large, heavy-bottom skillet. Add the onion and cook for 5 minutes, or until softened but not browned. Add the garlic and cook for an additional 30 seconds. Stir in the tomatoes and cook for 5 minutes, letting it bubble and stirring occasionally, until reduced to a thick mixture. Add the spinach leaves and cook, stirring, until they have wilted slightly. Season to taste with salt and pepper.

5 While the dough is rising, preheat the oven to 400°F/200°C.

Brush several baking sheets with olive oil. Turn the dough out onto a lightly floured counter and knead well for 2–3 minutes to knock out the air bubbles.

6 Roll out the dough very, very thinly and, using a 2 1/2-inch/ 6-cm plain, round cutter, cut out 32 circles. Place on the prepared baking sheets.

7 Spread each base with the spinach mixture to cover, then sprinkle the pine nuts over the top. Drizzle a little olive oil over each pizza. Bake in the preheated oven for 10–15 minutes, or until the edges of the dough are golden brown. Serve the spinach and tomato pizzas hot.

Chorizo Pizza

SERVES FOUR-SIX

6 tomatoes, sliced

2 onions, finely chopped

12 black olives

4 serrano ham slices

10 ready-to-eat chorizo
   sausage slices

2 tbsp chopped mixed fresh
   herbs

2 oz/55 g Tronchon or
   mozzarella cheese, thinly
   sliced

1/4 cup olive oil

salt and pepper

PIZZA BASE

1 package fresh yeast

1²/3 cups all-purpose flour,
   plus extra for dusting

1 cup lukewarm water

pinch of salt

1/4 cup olive oil

1 First make the pizza base. Mix the yeast with ¹/3 cup of the flour and the water in a bowl. Let stand for 10 minutes.

2 Meanwhile, sift the remaining flour with the salt into a large bowl and make a well in the center. Add the yeast mixture and the olive oil. Using an electric mixer, mix well for 5–10 minutes. Cover with a clean tea towel and let stand in a warm place until the dough has doubled in size.

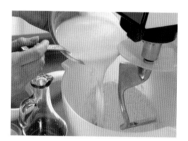

3 Preheat the oven to 425°F/220°C and place a baking sheet in the oven to warm. Pat out the pizza dough into an 11–12-inch/28–30-cm circle on a lightly floured counter and make a slightly raised rim around the edge.

4 Arrange the tomato slices on top of the pizza dough and season to taste with salt, then cover with the onion. Add the olives, ham, and chorizo, then season to taste with pepper and sprinkle over the herbs. Top with the cheese slices and drizzle with the olive oil.

5 Carefully transfer the pizza to the preheated baking sheet and bake in the preheated oven for 30 minutes, or until the cheese has melted and is bubbling and the rim has lightly browned. Cut into wedges and serve.